BAMA DYNASTY

THE CRIMSON TIDE'S ROAD TO COLLEGE FOOTBALL IMMORTALITY

Quarterback Tua Tagovailoa takes a snap from center Bradley Bozeman during the second half of the NCAA college football playoff championship game against Georgia.

This book is book is available in quantity at special discounts for your group or organization. For further information, contact:

Triumph Books LLC
814 North Franklin Street
Chicago, Illinois 60610
Phone: (312) 337-0747
www.triumphbooks.com

Printed in U.S.A.
ISBN: 978-1-62937-492-5

Content packaged by Mojo Media, Inc.
Joe Funk: Editor
Jason Hinman: Creative Director

All interior photos by AP Images

Front cover photo by AP Images
Back cover photo by USA TODAY Sports Images

CONTENTS

Acknowledgments 6

Introduction 8

College Football Playoff
Championship vs. Georgia 12

The Saban Dynasty 24

Alabama vs. Florida State 36

Alabama vs. Fresno State 42

Levi Wallace 46

Alabama vs. Colorado State 50

Alabama vs. Vanderbilt 54

Alabama vs. Ole Miss 58

Ronnie Clark 62

Alabama vs. Texas A&M 66

Alabama vs. Arkansas 72

Alabama vs. Tennessee 76

Running Game 82

Alabama vs. LSU 86

Alabama vs. Mississippi State 92

Rashaan Evans & Minkah Fitzpatrick 98

Alabama vs. Mercer 104

Iron Bowl vs. Auburn 108

Jalen Hurts 114

Sugar Bowl vs. Clemson 120

ACKNOWLEDGMENTS

A book like this doesn't get done without some serious effort by a lot of people, so special thanks to Noah Amstadter, Tom Bast, and everyone at Triumph Books who contributed.

Because it went to the printer the morning after Alabama's victory in the National Championship Game, I had to steal from myself — a lot.

So special thanks to everyone at SEC Country, especially Christopher Smith, Michael Carvell, and Ken Bradley, plus everyone who had a hand in editing any of my stories including Mike Bambach. SEC Country is part of the DieHards network, and a Verticals digital property of the Cox Media Group.

Except for Vanderbilt, the game stories are re-worked versions of what I wrote for SEC Country during the season, although in some cases what you see here only includes an excerpt. Regardless, if anything was used from a story that appears courtesy of SEC Country it is listed below.

The Saban Dynasty section was borrowed from two previous books of mine published by Triumph Books:
- *Nick Saban vs. College Football*, 2014
- *100 Things Crimson Tide Fans Should Know and Do Before They Die*, 2016 edition

Finally, as always, a special thanks to my wife Megan for her patience, support, and understanding, along with our daughter Evelyn, who was born the weekend of the Vanderbilt game. You can put two and two together on that one.

Game stories and excerpts:
- Introduction: "Alabama's Anthony Averett, Levi Wallace Are Tide's Version of Odd Couple," Oct. 27, 2017
- Game 1: "Message Sent: Alabama Still the King of College Football," Sept. 3, 2017
- Game 2: "Alabama's Offense Got What It Needed the Most Against Fresno State, a Confidence Boost," Sept. 10, 2017
- "From Walk-On to Reliable Corner, Levi Wallace Inspired by the Person Who Led Him to Alabama, His Late Father," Sept. 5, 2017
- Game 3: "Alabama's Beat-Up Defense Upset with Performance, but Help Is on the Way," Sept. 17, 2017
- Game 5: "Alabama Didn't Just Get Some Payback Against Ole Miss, but Set the Tone for the Rest of the Season," Sept. 30, 2017
- "Ronnie Clark's Return to the End Zone Was About a Lot More than Injury Comebacks," Oct. 6, 2017
- Game 6: "Alabama's Defense Ends Up Being the Difference as Alabama Tops Texas A&M 27-19," Oct. 7, 2017
- Game 7: "Alabama Feels Like It's Back on the Right Track with 41-9 Blowout Win Over Arkansas," Oct. 14, 2017
- Game 8: "Alabama's Defense Ready for Stretch Run, but Passing Game Must Improve," Oct. 21, 2017
- "One Way or Another, Alabama's Running Game Will Get Ya'," Oct. 19, 2017

DeVonta Smith's game-winning touchdown reception crowned another Crimson Tide season for the history books.

- Game 9: "Alabama Football's 24-10 Win Over LSU a Survival Test; Now, Rest of Season Is as Well," Nov. 4, 2017

- Game 10: "Alabama Finds Way to Do What It Couldn't in Title Game Last Year: Rally for Victory," Nov. 11, 2017

- "Alabama Defense's MVP (More Versatile Player): Rashaan Evans or Minkah Fitzpatrick?" Nov. 1, 2017

- Game 11: "Alabama's Senior Day Victory a Celebration for Players Such as Hootie Jones and His Mother," Nov. 18, 2017

- Game 12: "Alabama's Biggest Loss in Years Has Crimson Tide in Unfamiliar Territory," Nov. 25, 2017

- "Jalen Hurts' Homecoming Takes a Back Seat to Alabama's Goal at Texas A&M, Winning," Oct. 5, 2017; and "Alabama and Jalen Hurts Relishing Having Another Chance, Both in the CFP and at Clemson," Dec. 17, 2017

Stories from the College Football Playoff may also be courtesy of SEC Country. ■

INTRODUCTION

It was a very unusual season for the University of Alabama football program.

It again came very close to running the table, advanced to the College Football Playoff for the fourth straight time, and had its dynasty on the line when it faced Clemson yet again, this time in the Sugar Bowl semifinal.

That all really wasn't anything new.

Nick Saban's incredible run continued, with the coach posting record after record.

For example, Alabama had defeated 73 consecutive unranked opponents. It nearly scored in every quarter of every game, as the string of 49 consecutive quarters extended from the previous College Football Playoff semifinal against Washington to the regular-season finale. The senior class finished the regular season with 51 wins over a four-year period, tying the NCAA record set by the 2016 Crimson Tide senior class.

But what really stood out about this particular Crimson Tide team were two things: its resiliency, especially considering all the injuries at the linebacker position, and that the players were just, well, likable.

From captains Bradley Bozeman, Rashaan Evans, Minkah Fitzpatrick, and Shaun Dion Hamilton on down, the Crimson Tide did a lot of things that were too often overlooked, and we're not talking about Fitzpatrick winning the Chuck Bednarik Award for defensive player of the year or becoming the first Saban-coached player to win the Thorpe Award for best defensive back.

Rather, things like Fitzpatrick giving his spare time to numerous local organizations including the local YMCA and TAP Inc. (the nonprofit youth athlete assistance program designed to prepare athletes to be successful in the life outside of athletics). He also spent his spring break with a group of Alabama student-athletes as part of mission trip to do relief work in Costa Rica.

This was someone who in high school lost his home to a hurricane and subsequently helped his father at work. Yet he declined interview requests to talk about the trip, not wanting to be singled out for trying to lend a helping hand when the attention should be on those who needed it.

Senior punter JK Scott also spent extensive time working with youth groups, and Bozeman reached out to help a terminally ill cancer patient and his family. Numerous players visited Cameron Pruitt, a 13-year old boy who had been fighting cancer for eight years. When he died, sophomore quarterback Jalen Hurts wrote the words "Cam Strong" and "RIP Cam," on his wristbands during the Ole Miss game.

"I built a relationship with him," Hurts said. "I always gave him my earrings. I always gave him a little sweat band I have and I wear just to show him we're playing for him and he's on my mind for sure."

Hurts also wore a wristband for 10-year-old Aubreigh Nicholas who was suffering from a rare and inoperable brain cancer known as DIPG. A photo of Saban kissing her on the head before a game went viral.

Perhaps a better way to explain what this team was about could be found with the starting cornerbacks.

Anthony Averett was from New Jersey, while

Linebacker Shaun Dion Hamilton hoists the National Championship Trophy after Alabama's hard-fought, overtime victory over Georgia.

Levi Wallace hailed from Arizona. The roommates weren't mega-recruits. They didn't trash talk like many cornerbacks. They even wore atypical numbers, although ones Alabama has had success with before. The best player to wear Averett's No. 28 was probably Don McNeal (1977-79) or Javier Arenas (2006-09), while defensive end E.J. Junior (1977-80) previously sported Wallace's No. 39. They were All-Americans.

They had big seasons, yet most Crimson Tide fans wouldn't recognize either on the street — some would only figure it out if they were with Fitzpatrick.

"I've got more Instagram followers," Wallace said about how his life changed.

He was being modest. It's kind of odd for a cornerback, but that's how these guys were. Meanwhile, not only did they draw attention from NFL scouts and various evaluation services, but the term "shutdown" was occasionally murmured.

"I don't know about all that," Wallace said. "They got a couple of catches on me this season. To be a lockdown corner, you have to be like Darrelle Revis or Richard Sherman, where quarterbacks are afraid to even come your way.

"Like Ant. He doesn't have too many passes thrown his way. I think he's one of the best corners in college football."

Statistically, both were top-notch, and Alabama's defense was again in its usual spot of being considered the best in the nation. Under the direction of coordinator Jeremy Pruitt, the Crimson Tide challenged to lead the nation in all four major statistical categories: Rushing, pass-efficiency, scoring, and total defense.

That's despite all the injuries, and there were a lot of them.

The cornerbacks were also a part of an extremely experienced secondary, with the six primary starters (including the nickel and dime packages) all seniors or juniors.

"It makes a big difference," Averett said about having such a veteran group after having nearly the exact opposite the previous couple of seasons. "It's like the roles flipped with us this year."

When Averett was recruited in the Class of 2013, he carried a consensus 4-star rating, but there was more buzz about other players.

"Anthony's like a lot of guys that didn't really ever play the position in high school," Saban said. "I think it takes a little longer for them to develop if they ever play a new position, especially if you take a guy from offense to defense. We recruited Anthony because of his athleticism, his speed."

Wallace was considered more of a project as he walked on in January of his freshman year in 2014.

"I think the key to Levi's success is the diligence he sort of goes about his work with," Saban said. "He worked hard to improve and get bigger and stronger. He's a real technician as a player, very smart, instinctive guy."

Averett became a starter in 2016, but even after Marlon Humphrey left a year early for the National Football League, Wallace was still considered a reserve. He kept plugging away and pushing during fall camp. He didn't start the season opener against Florida State, but after being inserted the defense responded and didn't yield another point.

The Florida State game was a turning point for Averett as well, because the Seminoles went after him with little success. He subsequently started to notice opponents challenging him less, which for a cornerback can be the ultimate compliment.

It's a show of respect.

That's the bottom line when it comes to the 2017 Crimson Tide, which won Alabama's 17th national championship and Saban's sixth overall, respect. This team earned every bit of it over an incredibly difficult season. ∎

The 2017 season marked Nick Saban's sixth national championship as a head coach and his fifth with the Crimson Tide.

ALABAMA 26, GEORGIA 23 (OT)

JANUARY 8, 2018 · ATLANTA, GEORGIA

CRIMSON PRIDE

Freshmen Lead Crimson Tide to Stunning Comeback Win Over Bulldogs

The emotions were all on display on the floor at Mercedes-Benz Stadium.

Laughing; crying. Joy; shock. Pride; disbelief.

That was Alabama football team after it pulled off maybe the most stunning, incredible and unbelievable national championship game ever seen. So many words could be used to describe it, yet none of them were good enough.

"Best feeling in the world," was all senior cornerback Levi Wallace could offer while quietly watching the Crimson Tide fans celebrate their 17th national title. "Nothing like it."

Nor was this game, which one simply had to watch to fully understand. After a horrendous first half for the Crimson Tide, in which the offense managed just 21 passing yards and no points, Nick Saban pretty much turned his team over to his true freshman and asked them to win the national championship against Georgia.

As incredible and improbable as that sounds, they did.

It was more than Tua Tagovailoa at quarterback, who sparked the offense after Jalen Hurts was pulled at halftime. Wide receiver Devonta Smith caught the winning touchdown in overtime. Running back Najee Harris led the ground attack and Alex Leatherwood was at left tackle after sophomore starter Jonah Williams left the game with an injury.

There was also a missed field goal at the end of regulation, and Tagovailoa was sacked on the play before he threw the 41-yard touchdown pass down the left sideline. That's what kind of a whirlwind it was with Alabama pulling out the dramatic 26-23 victory.

There was even a postgame marriage proposal by senior center Bradley Bozeman (she said yes).

Meanwhile, lost in the excitement was Saban winning his sixth national championship, his fifth over the last nine seasons at Alabama. He tied Paul "Bear" Bryant for the most ever, but three by the legend were considered spilt titles including the controversial 1973 title when the coaches' poll named the Crimson Tide No. 1 before it lost to Notre Dame.

When it comes to dynasties, though, there's no longer any doubt that this is the greatest that college football has ever seen. Miami (1983-92) and Notre Dame (1941-50) can both claim four titles over a 10-year period, but neither was able to maintain it, or stay

PLAY OF THE GAME:
The 41-yard touchdown pass from quarterback Tua Tagovailoa to wide receiver DeVonta Smith in overtime will have Alabama fans singing The Who song "The Kids Are Alright" for a long time about the freshmen.

Calvin Ridley celebrates his fourth quarter touchdown catch, one of his four catches for 32 yards in the Alabama win.

PLAYER OF THE GAME:

Tagovailoa came off the bench to throw three touchdowns passes and lead the crazy comeback against Georgia in its backyard of Atlanta. He was 14-for-24 for 166 yards and also ran for 47 more before factoring in two sacks for minus-20 yards.

on top with this kind of consistency.

"This is a great win, a team win," Saban said. "Someone tried to give me a game ball. I don't think you give anybody a game ball. It has to be a team ball, and that's exactly what we'll do with it."

But no one was talking about that after the game, or that how Saban was arguably two plays away, against Clemson a year earlier and the Kick Six game in 2013, from having two more titles.

This was oh-so-close to being a third near-miss, only Alabama rallied in the second half from down 13-0. Tagovailoa's first possession didn't go anywhere, but his second did as four straight completions peaked with freshman Henry Ruggs III snaring a 6-yard touchdown.

Alabama seemed to finally be on its way, but Georgia quickly countered with a controversial 80-yard touchdown pass to Mecole Hardman, who had fans and officials zooming in to try and see if he stepped out of bounds at the 16.

It could have ended Alabama, especially when Tagovailoa answered with an interception on a play where there was a missed signal. Yet somehow it didn't.

Not the team that had lost so many players to injuries, and had gotten to back into the College Football Playoff.

The comeback was anything but pretty. It seemed like after junking the original game plan offensive coordinator Brian Daboll was all but diagramming plays in the artificial turf. A key turnover in the second half happened when a pass deflected off senior defensive end Da'Shawn Hand's head and to sophomore lineman Raekwon Davis for an interception.

Freshman running back Najee Harris provided a late spark for the Crimson Tide, running for 64 yards on just six carries.

STAT OF THE GAME:

After being outgained 333-191 through three quarters, including 225-75 in the air, Alabama had an edge of 155-41 in total offense yards while tying the game up in the fourth quarter. They then won in overtime.

"All I know is that it hit my hand and I caught it," Davis said. "It was crazy, but I did it. I didn't know I could run like that."

He returned it 19 yards to help set up an Andy Pappanastos 43-yard field goal to bring Alabama within 20-10.

But the fourth quarter was all Alabama. A 71-yard drive resulted in a 30-yard field goal, and with the defense forcing a three-and-out, a 66-yard drive resulted in a 7-yard touchdown catch by junior wide receiver Calvin Ridley — who until that point had been outperformed by his brother Riley, who had six catches for 82 yards for Georgia.

Tied at 20, Alabama had a golden chance to win the game after the defense forced another three-and-out, with Tagovailoa leading a drive from his own 35 and putting Alabama in place to win in the final seconds. Only the 26-yard attempt sailed wide left.

Georgia, which beat Oklahoma in double-overtime at the Rose Bowl to advance, could only get a field goal during its turn in the extra frame. The Bulldogs thought they were on the cusp of victory following the sack, only to see the perfect throw into the end zone.

"When they called the play I looked at Tua and I said, 'Trust me,'" said Smith, as the team that lost in the final second the previous year was both dumbfounded and overjoyed when it sort of turned the tables.

"I think everyone had turned their TVs off," said junior defensive lineman Isaiah Buggs, who didn't know yet that President Donald Trump had left the game at halftime.

"This is amazing," exhausted senior linebacker Rashaan Evans said while slumped in front of this locker. "We went through so much."

Defensive lineman D'Shawn Hand delivers a shot to Georgia quarterback Jake Fromm. The freshman quarterback completed only 16 of 32 passes and threw an interception to go with two touchdown passes.

"They said we weren't supposed to be here," junior running back Damien Harris yelled. "Now look."

That was after Harris had shed a few tears on the field only to later run out of the locker room yelling to reporters, "I love you. I love all of you. Thank you!"

He didn't care that Alabama had outgained Georgia on the ground 184-133, or that his offense had only converted 3 of 14 third-down opportunities. Tagovailoa going 14-for-24 for 166 yards raised a lot of questions about the quarterback position moving forward, but those were things to be figured out another day, along with how Saban might be able to top this.

"We're national champions!" Davis screamed into the night. "We're No. 1." ■

Opposite: Tua Tagovailoa charges a hole against the Georgia defense. Tagovailoa used both his athleticism running the ball and accuracy throwing the ball to spark Alabama's offense to the dramatic win. Above: Georgia running back Nick Chubb gets washed over by the Crimson Tide defenders. The senior tailback had only 25 yards on 18 carries.

DeVonta Smith's overtime touchdown catch was a shocking end to an unforgettable game, and sure to go down as one of the most incredible moments in Crimson Tide history.

TAGOVAILOA IGNITES ALABAMA OFFENSE

True Freshman Comes Off Bench, Passes for Three TDs in Comeback Win

It was the call that Nick Saban had to make. Down 13 points at the half, his offense was more than struggling, it was stagnant. Four straight three-and-outs, and going 1-for-6 on third-down conversions, had put his team in a vast hole, and Alabama had just 21 passing yards against Georgia in the National Championship Game.

"We needed a spark," Saban said.

To ignite one, he benched the 2016 SEC Offensive Player of the Year, a quarterback who was 25-2 as a starter. With sophomore Jalen Hurts watching from the sideline, Saban inserted true freshman quarterback Tua Tagovailoa into probably the most high-pressure situation imaginable in college football.

It ended up winning him and the Crimson Tide another national championship.

With Tagovailoa completing 14 of 24 passes for 166 yards and three touchdowns, Alabama pulled out a dramatic 26-23 overtime victory at Mercedes-Benz Stadium.

"We've had this in our mind that if we were struggling offensively, we would give Tua an opportunity, even in the last game," Saban said. "No disrespect to Jalen, but the real thought was that, you know, they came into the game thinking we were going to run the ball and be able to run quarterback runs, which we made a couple of explosive plays on. But with the absence of a passing game and being able to make explosive plays and being able to convert on third down, I just didn't feel we could run the ball well enough.

"I thought Tua would give us a better chance."

Coming in, Alabama's offense had struggled in November, especially in the loss at Auburn, and again against No. 1 Clemson in the Sugar Bowl. When Hurts had missed a couple of days of practice due to illness, Tagovailoa filled in and looked good.

At first it didn't look like he would be able to replicate that. Tagovailoa's first possession went nowhere, and two plays after Georgia regained the momentum and went up 20-10 on an 80-yard touchdown, he threw what could have been a back-breaking interception.

"The issue was we missed a signal," Saban said. "In other words, everybody was running a running play, and he thought it was a passing play. So it causes a problem when all the receivers are blocking instead of running a pass route, and then it sort of quadruples the problem when the quarterback throws to him anyway.

"But we learn from those things, right?"

"Yes sir," Tagovaiola responded during the postgame press conference.

After Hurts completed 3 of 8 passes, Tagovailoa had touchdown strikes to three receivers: freshman Henry Ruggs III, junior Calvin Ridley, and freshman DeVonta Smith to lead the comeback. The last for 41 yards was the game-winner.

"Smitty was wide open," said Tagovailoa, the offensive player of the game. Junior defensive tackle Da'Ron Payne landed the defensive honor.

As for Hurts, he was supportive and answered every question from reporters in front of his locker after the game.

"That's what teammates do," he said. ∎

Freshman quarterback Tua Tagovailoa was exactly the boost that the Alabama offense needed, passing for three touchdowns and becoming a Bama legend in just over a half of football.

DEFINING A DYNASTY

Saban Era Ranks Among Greatest in College Football History

What's a dynasty in college football? It's generally considered three championships in six years, although even that's not as clear-cut as most fans would expect. There are different definitions by era, as there weren't that many programs in existence before the polls were created, and subsequently most titles were shared until the Bowl Championship Series and College Football Playoff were devised.

Not surprisingly, the game's most dominant programs all arguably came before the poll era began in 1936, including Yale (1874-1909), Michigan (1901-05), and Notre Dame (1918-30).

Since the advent of the Associated Press college football poll, there have essentially been four different types of dynasties over the years, with some obviously more legitimate than others.

For your core dynasties, featuring programs that dominated for multiple seasons or years, you're talking Army (1944-50), when many of the best athletes enlisted and transfer rules were waived during World War II, Florida State (1987-2000), Penn State (1967-70) and Southern California (1962-72).

Asterisk dynasties, those influenced by NCAA penalties, include Miami (1983-94), Oklahoma (1971-80), and, most recently, Southern California (2002-08).

True dynasties, which meet the standard of three championships over a span of six years, are made up of two by Paul "Bear" Bryant (1961-66 and 1971-80), Nebraska under Tom Osborne (1993-97) and Oklahoma (1948-58) during Bud Wilkinson's reign.

All are impressive, but the pure dynasties are the ones that really stand out. Not only did the programs win at least three consensus championships over a span of six years or less, but they also faced quality competition.

Only three programs belong in this exclusive club: Minnesota under Bernie Bierman (1934-41), Notre Dame under Frank Leahy (1941-49), and Alabama under Nick Saban.

Alabama has accomplished this while facing tougher opposition, if only because players are considered bigger and faster nowadays. For many years it wasn't uncommon to see a team win the national championship while only playing a couple of ranked opponents.

Alabama faced six in 2009, five in 2011 and six in 2012. It set a record with nine in 2015, and played 10 ranked opponents in 2016 but lost the title game.

Yet the dynasty has continued …

With five national championships in a span of nine seasons, Nick Saban's tenure at Alabama ranks amongst the greatest dynasties in college football history.

DEFINING A DYNASTY

2009

As football seasons go, it was quite an ending.

The setting: The Rose Bowl, where the University of Alabama football program first made a name for itself in the 1920s and won its early national championships.

The opponent: Texas, which the Crimson Tide had never defeated before in eight attempts including five bowl games.

The prize: Much more than a crystal football.

At stake was an end to years of anxiety, wondering if the program's rollercoaster would ever stop, a lot of mediocrity, being two years removed from playing in back-to-back Independence Bowls, and lingering doubt as to whether one of the most storied programs in history would ever be able to reclaim its proud status.

"We back," sophomore running back Mark Ingram proudly said after the decisive 37-21 victory in the BCS National Championship Game.

With four turnovers created by the defense, which also knocked Longhorns senior quarterback Colt McCoy out of the game with a shoulder injury, and both Ingram and freshman running back Trent Richardson tallying more than 100 rushing yards, the Crimson Tide celebrated in the same place where it won its first crown 84 years before in similar fashion against Washington.

But never before had an Alabama or Southeastern Conference team gone 14-0 to win the title, much less beat the previous three national champions along the way. The program's first Heisman Trophy and second Butkus Award (Derrick Thomas, 1988) were nice bonuses.

Alabama won its 13th title by doing what it does best, playing physically, despite numerous injuries including quarterback Greg McElroy having cracked ribs. Ingram and Richardson gashed and grinded away at the nation's No. 1 defense against the run, with Alabama more than doubling in the first half what Texas

had allowed per game (62.2 yards).

Also reaching the end zone was defensive lineman Marcell Dareus in spectacular fashion. After Texas took a timeout with 15 seconds remaining, he snared the subsequent shovel pass off a deflection and made a spin move before running over Texas freshman quarterback Garrett Gilbert.

"My first reaction was grab the ball, and then after that I blanked out," said Dareus, who scored the 28-yard touchdown just three seconds before halftime. "All I was thinking about is Mark Ingram and Javier (Arenas) and just doing moves I didn't think I could do."

Although Alabama had scored 24 unanswered points, Texas wasn't ready to concede and was able to pull within three points in the fourth quarter before the Tide got to Gilbert again. A fake blitz left senior linebacker Eryk Anders unblocked, and he caught the quarterback on his blind side to force the ball loose with sophomore linebacker Courtney Upshaw recovering the fumble at the Texas 3. Ingram punched in the touchdown, and Richardson another for the new kings of college football.

"It is really difficult to express just how proud I am," Director of Athletics Mal Moore said. "This team, these coaches and in particular Coach Saban, the effort he's put into this program in the three years he's been here, and to reach this level and this peak, and win the national championship, is quite remarkable. I think it's just so fitting that we were honored to play in the Rose Bowl for the national championship and win it here."

Texas outgained Alabama 276-263 yards, was more successful on third downs and notched five sacks against a unit that had yielded only 15 all season. None of that mattered. Ingram was named the game's offensive MVP and Dareus took home the defensive award despite having just the interception and one tackle — when what appeared to be a routine hit ended McCoy's collegiate career. They, along with senior guard Mike Johnson,

Mark Ingram signals to the crowd after scoring a touchdown in the fourth quarter of Alabama's win over Texas in the BCS Championship game. The 2009 Heisman Trophy winner gained 116 yards on 22 carries and scored two touchdowns in Alabama's 37-21 win.

DEFINING A DYNASTY

kissed and cradled the crystal football when it was handed to them on the victory platform.

"I feel like I've played an entire career, it's been one heck of a season," McElroy said. "This team is just so special. I've been a part of a lot of great things. I've been in a lot of football locker rooms, a lot of hockey locker rooms and things like that, but this team has the heart.

"That's what it is, willingness to go the extra mile."

A few days later, the 2009 Crimson Tide gathered to celebrate one final time with 38,000 fans at Bryant-Denny Stadium. It featured tributes, speeches and hardware — a whole lot of hardware.

The loudest cheers came when Saban asked for fans to stand and give the team its biggest ovation yet, which they gratefully obliged, but also when he set a new goal: For the Crimson Tide to have the most consistent winning program in the nation.

"I want everyone here to know this is not the end," he said. "This is the beginning."

2011

When it comes to Nick Saban's third national championship, second with Alabama, there were two things that can't be avoided or overlooked.

The first was Alabama's ability to overcome adversity, and we're not talking about sustaining a loss, the disappointment of the previous season, or dealing with the kinds of things that usually come up in a competitive environment. Instead, it got an overdose of tragedy during the months building up to the 2011 season.

Mere days after the annual A-Day scrimmage in April, and the unveiling of Saban's statue along the "Walk of Champions" for winning the 2009 national title, a series of horrific tornados struck the state including one that went through the heart of Tuscaloosa. Then in May, reserve offensive lineman Aaron Douglas was found

dead on a balcony the morning after attending a party in Jacksonville, Florida, which the Nassau County medical examiner's office would rule an accident. He was 21.

Despite all that, and a 9-6 overtime loss to LSU at Bryant-Denny Stadium on November 5th, Alabama managed to reach the BCS National Championship Game without playing for its own conference title.

The other thing the 2011 Crimson Tide will always be remembered for is its unbelievable defense. Although running back Trent Richardson was a Heisman Trophy finalist who set the Alabama single-season rushing record, and after moving from right guard to left tackle Barrett Jones became the third player in program history to win the Outland Trophy (college football's best interior lineman). The defense led the nation in every major statistical category.

"I love competitors," Saban said. "I think that there's a lot of talent on this defensive team, but I tell you what, these guys are great competitors and they're warriors, and sometimes they can't practice very well all week and I get mad at them. But, man, when they go to play, they play hard. They play well together. And they have a lot of pride in their performance, in what they do, and they've done it extremely well. Statistically, they've done it better than probably any group we've ever had."

Specifically, it was No. 1 in pass-efficiency defense (83.69 rating), pass defense (111.46 yards per game), rushing defense (72.15), scoring defense (8.15 points), and total defense (183.62 yards per game) — in addition to third-down defense, red-zone defense, first downs allowed, and three-and-outs — and all by wide margins.

He added: "You throw the ball out, they're going to go get it, because they are a hateful bunch and they are as competitive as you can ever imagine, and I think that's probably why they played really well in big games."

None was bigger than the rematch with LSU in New Orleans, where the Alabama defense dominated for a 21-0 victory and the only shutout in any BCS bowl.

Nick Saban argues with a referee during Alabama's game against North Texas on September 17, 2011. Saban remained focused and intense during his third championship season.

DEFINING A DYNASTY

Led by the game's defensive MVP Courtney Upshaw, who had seven tackles and a sack, Alabama finished with a 21-5 edge in first downs, 69-44 in plays, and 384-92 in total yards. LSU's longest possession went just 23 yards and its biggest play was for 19. It went three-and-out six times, with an interception by linebacker C.J. Mosley on the second play of a possession, and converted just two third-down opportunities.

LSU crossed the 50-yard line only once, and then promptly went backwards and fumbled away the ball. By comparison, Alabama failed to cross midfield only twice, one of which resulted in a punt from the 46, as it chiseled away its 14th national title.

"I've never coached a team that was more determined, more dedicated to overcoming adversity than this group of guys," Saban said after getting another Gatorade treatment. "I've never seen a more dominant performance than what they did in the national championship game against LSU."

In addition to Alabama winning its second crystal football in three years, Alabama was also presented with the Disney Spirit Award that annually goes to college football's most inspirational player, team or figure.

"It's awesome," long-snapper Carson Tinker said. "There are no words that can describe this. Just a lot of work paid off. Everyone here faced some kind of adversity, and just to see how they all came out of that is a great thing."

2012

There were roughly two minutes remaining in the game and Alabama senior offensive lineman Barrett Jones knew that the time was finally at hand. He grabbed co-captain Damion Square and went for a Gatorade jug, while teammates formed a wall behind Coach Nick Saban.

They subsequently executed the dousing to perfection, which was fitting considering what the Crimson Tide had just done to Notre Dame — dominating from the start and crushing the previously unbeaten Fighting Irish in the BCS Championship Game, 42-14.

"I'm not a really emotional guy, but I really enjoyed the moment," Jones said after Alabama won its 15th national title and second straight.

"It's been amazing. I just can't really put it into words right now."

That was a strong sentiment among teammates as well as they tried to put it into perspective what had been accomplished.

With the victory, Alabama become college football's first back-to-back consensus national champion since Nebraska in 1994-95, as well as the first school to win three national titles in the BCS era — never mind in four years.

Outside of the Cornhuskers one had to go all the way back to Notre Dame in the late 1940s to find a comparison, and those Irish teams didn't play postseason games.

Saban also went from being the first coach to lift the crystal trophy a third time, to enjoying his fourth (three at Alabama). In the modern era of the game, only Paul W. "Bear" Bryant (six) and Knute Rockne (five) had more national titles, and many of theirs weren't considered consensus.

They were, however, two of the few coaches who had pulled off back-to-back national titles.

"Regardless of the result that this team achieved, they certainly exceeded every expectation that we had for them with the number of guys we graduated last year, the number of new roles, young players, injuries, the adversity that this team had to overcome," Saban said. "These guys really battled.

"People talk about how the most difficult thing is to

Alabama linebacker Nico Johnson knocks Michigan quarterback Denard Robinson off his feet during the Crimson Tide's 41-14 win over the Wolverines in the 2012 season opener at Cowboys Stadium.

DEFINING A DYNASTY

win your first championship. Really the most difficult is to win the next one, because there's always a feeling of entitlement, and the commitment that these guys made two days after we played LSU last year in the national championship game to be a team, to set a goal to accomplish something of significance is really special for what they were able to accomplish."

Moreover, the win was the Southeastern Conference's seventh straight national championship while Alabama finally vanquished one of its demons, beating the nemesis that cost it the 1973 title among others indirectly.

"It's unbelievable, I really can't say anything," senior long-snapper Carson Tinker tried to explain.

"We wanted to do something no one else has done. I think we did we it tonight. Unprecedented. That's the word that's been in my head the last month or so."

Midway through the second quarter Notre Dame's bench was silent and stunned at the Crimson Tide's proficiency on both sides of the ball.

Notre Dame's defense had given up just nine points in the first quarter, and two rushing touchdowns all season; Alabama posted 14 points on its first two possessions and reached the end zone a third time on its first play of the second quarter.

The Fighting Irish was thought to have the nation's best red-zone defense; The Crimson Tide scored touchdowns on all five possessions inside the 20.

Only one opposing running back had reached 100-rushing yards against Notre Dame; Junior Eddie Lacy had 96 in the first half including a show-stopping spin move into the end zone for an 11-yard touchdown reception.

Lacy finished with 145 rushing yards on 20 carries, and similar to Mark Ingram Jr. and Trent Richardson in the 2009 title game against Texas the Crimson Tide enjoyed two 100-yard rushing performances with freshman T.J. Yeldon finishing with 108 yards on 21 carries.

Destiny? Luck of the Irish? Alabama thumbed its zone at all that and then un-mercilessly squashed previously unbeaten leprechauns. Notre Dame won the coin toss and nothing else.

"We said we're coming to take it, and we're not leaving here until we get it," said junior tackle D.J. Fluker, who would often tell his collegiate teammates, "Play like they took your lunch money."

2015

In Nick Saban's words, the 2015 Alabama football team was all but "dead and buried" by media and the rest of the college football world. At least that's what he was portraying to his team after an early-season loss that essentially made every subsequent Saturday an elimination game regarding its national title hopes.

Only the Crimson Tide responded.

With the defense and running game leading the way, Alabama did what the two previous teams could not, run the table, successfully defending its Southeastern Conference title and then surviving the College Football Playoff for the program's 16th national championship.

"This is my — I hate to say it — favorite team because I love 'em all," Saban said. "These guys have come so far and have done so much. Their will, their spirit to compete and do the kind of kind of things they needed to do to be the kind of team they could be, I'm happy for them.

"This is all about winning a game for them. It's great for our fans. It's great for the state of Alabama, but I wanted to win this game for these guys."

With the 45-40 victory against Clemson at the site of the Fiesta Bowl (giving Alabama under Saban a grand slam at what used to be the four Bowl Championship Series locations) the debate could really begin on if Saban was the greatest coach in college football history,

Alabama running back Derrick Henry carries the ball during the College Football Playoff National Championship game against Clemson. Henry won the Heisman Trophy in 2015, setting an SEC record with 2,219 rushing yards and 28 touchdowns on 395 carries.

DEFINING A DYNASTY

and if Alabama's ongoing dynasty was the best the game had ever seen.

The crown was Saban's fifth, four with the Crimson Tide, which became the first program during the modern era to win four titles over a seven-year span.

Additionally, it was Saban's sixth victory against a team ranked No. 1, while no one else in college football history had more than four (Lou Holtz, Jimmy Johnson, and Jack Mollenkopf. Paul W. "Bear" Bryant was among those with three), and Alabama extended its streak of being No. 1 at some point in a season to an incredible eight straight years.

Regardless, after both semifinals were blowouts, with Alabama defeating Michigan State 38-0 in the Cotton Bowl, the championship more than made up for it and would be remembered as one of the best title games ever played. The two teams combined for 1,023 yards and it still went down to the end.

Junior running back Derrick Henry rushed for 158 yards on 36 carries and scored three touchdowns while becoming Alabama's all-time leading rusher. Despite being sacked five times senior quarterback Jake Coker had a career high 335 yards on 16 of 25 attempts, and no turnovers.

Overshadowing both was the game's offensive MVP, junior tight end O.J. Howard, who had a historic performance with five receptions for 208 yards and touchdowns of 51 and 53 yards.

"O.J., quite honestly, should have been more involved all year long," Saban said. "Sometimes he was open and we didn't get him the ball, but I think the last two games have been breakout games for him in terms of what he's capable of and what he can do.

"I would say that it's bad coaching on my part that he didn't have the opportunity to do that all year long."

Alabama also pulled off a jaw-dropping onside kick when the game was tied 24-24 with just under 11 minutes remaining, when Adam Griffith perfectly bounced the football into open space and redshirt freshman Marlon Humphrey made a leaping catch to the dismay of Clemson coach Dabo Swinney — a walk-on receiver on Alabama's 1992 national championship team.

Alabama's run was even more impressive when you consider the brutal schedule that began with a neutral-site game against Wisconsin, and included the top three teams from the SEC East: Florida, Tennessee and Georgia.

Overall, Alabama played nine opponents that were ranked at the time, the most of any national champion. Every team in the division not only finished with a winning record, but at some point of the season was ranked — a first in college football. Combined, the SEC West went 31-4 against non-conference opponents, and 13-2 against the SEC East.

"To face 12 straight elimination games after the Ole Miss [loss]," Saban said. "The resiliency, the competitive character that this team showed at being able to do that, and even coming back from behind in the national championship game really shows the spirit that made this team something special." ∎

Alabama defenders smother Wisconsin running back Corey Clement during the Crimson Tide's 35-17 win over the Badgers on September 5, 2015.

ALABAMA 24, FLORIDA STATE 7

SEPTEMBER 2, 2017 · ATLANTA, GEORGIA

THE KING IS BACK

Crimson Tide Humbles Florida State and ACC in Season Opener

It was as if they were openly asking: "When will they learn?"

After a whole offseason of hearing coaches, especially from the Atlantic Coast Conference, crow about how their league was the best, the University of Alabama football team responded in the only way it knows how with a resolving win.

Coming in, No. 3 Florida State was considered one of the best teams in the nation, with all the necessary ingredients to challenge for a spot in the College Football Playoff, if not more. Yet the Seminoles left more than limping.

It wasn't just because of the 24-7 score or how quarterback Deondre Francois had to be carried and then carted off after suffering a season-ending knee injury — ironically on a hit by the Tallahassee-based player Florida State didn't offer a scholarship, safety Ronnie Harrison.

Equally damaging was how the Seminoles lost. No one left new Mercedes-Benz Stadium thinking that Florida State might eventually be the better team or deserved to win the game.

They left believing Alabama is still Alabama and the SEC is still the SEC.

"I love playing against SEC schools," Florida State junior center Alec Eberle said. "They tend to have the bigger dudes and better defenses. It is really fun to go out and compete against the best players in the country."

Some of the coaches in his league, and even his own school president who was quoted as saying "I shouldn't talk too much trash, but I think we're gonna beat Alabama pretty bad," needed to take note after poking the Crimson Tide numerous times during the buildup. As representatives of institutions for higher learning they should have known better.

A lot of the game statistics ended up being pretty even, but Alabama did a lot of things that top-notch teams do.

It made the biggest plays. It didn't turn the ball over. It answered.

For example, when FSU made an impressive 90-yard touchdown drive, Alabama quickly came back with a 53-yard strike to junior wide receiver Calvin Ridley.

It found ways to win, which was the one ingredient lacking in the team's previous game, the last-second loss to Clemson in the National Championship Game.

"You could always pick out a few things that were a little ugly, but I'm really proud of the way they competed," Nick Saban said. "They played really hard in the game."

Linebacker Rashaan Evans returns a blocked field goal. Evans had a part in several key special teams plays that propelled Alabama to a 24-7 victory over Florida State.

PLAY OF THE GAME:
The punt block in the third quarter completely changed the momentum of the game. Followed by three straight turnovers, Florida State had just 20 yards of total offense thereafter.

PLAYER OF THE GAME:

Damien Harris. The junior running back had the huge punt block, averaged 8.1 yards per rushing attempt and scored a touchdown on an 11-yard carry.

For eight months Alabama had sat and stewed about the title-game loss in Tampa. Considering the pride involved, the talent on the roster and both the program's and Saban's history no one should have expected anything less in the matchup hailed the Greatest Opener of All Time.

Yet Alabama felt it didn't play that well.

"Sloppy," was how Ridley described it. "We can play a lot better."

Special teams were crucial, but also had issues. There were some uncharacteristic early defensive breakdowns. The offensive line had a rough night going up against a very good, fast FSU defense, especially in pass protection.

"I give a lot of respect to them," sophomore quarterback Jalen Hurts said.

Alabama didn't find its offensive identity, which will result in taking another long look at the right tackle spot. Cornerback was still a question mark as converted wide receiver Trevon Diggs was hoped to be the long-term solution but FSU struggled to move the ball after former walk-on Levi Wallace was inserted. At linebacker, Alabama had four major injuries, with Christian Miller and Terrell Lewis possibly done for the season.

That this team overcame all that probably scared the rest of college football just like massive defensive lineman Raekwon Davis' monster sack that would have caused nearly anyone to scream like Chris Tucker in the movie "The Fifth Element."

It came a week after he was struck by a bullet in the leg. Maybe if it had been a bazooka he would have missed a couple of weeks.

Bo Scarbrough runs for a chunk of the 173 rushing yards Alabama produced in the victory against Florida State.

STAT OF THE GAME:

Alabama's average field position in the second half was at the Florida State 38-yard line. Also, Nick Saban improved to 11-0 against his former assistant coaches

The point is, no one was questioning his or the Crimson Tide's resolve.

Alabama had to use numerous players who really had no business being on the field yet and still pushed around the Seminoles. Florida State couldn't run the ball, really pieced together just one sustained drive after the first quarter and was physically punished beginning with the bone-crushing hit by freshman Daniel Wright (also recruited out of the Sunshine State) on special teams.

"The young guys came through" said linebacker Shaun Dion Hamilton, who had a team-high eight tackles including 3.5 for a loss in his first game back from a torn ACL in the 2016 SEC Championship Game.

Nevertheless, while Clemson was the reigning national champion, the path to the crown still went through both the Crimson Tide and the SEC.

That's what led to the chanting "S-E-C, S-E-C," which was sort of like people in the Deep South politely saying, "Bless their heart" when someone says something stupid.

As for the team, it simply did its talking on the field and the message was simple: Alabama's still the king of college football. ∎

Part of a defensive effort that limited Florida State to 250 total yards, Anthony Averett (top) and Shyheim Carter (bottom) tackle Seminoles wide receiver Nyqwan Murray.

A STEPPING STONE

Alabama Wins 66th Straight Against an Unranked Opponent

Forget the score. It ended up being 41-10, but it really didn't matter.

Alabama was going to win and everyone knew it. Fresno State was a team with a new coach, coming off a 1-11 season and trying to find its way. The Crimson Tide needed just two snaps to show the difference between playing Incarnate Word, a sub-par FCS team the Bulldogs manhandled the previous Saturday, and facing the No. 1 team in the nation.

On paper, the contrast was about 100 points. It could have been more had Alabama been more motivated, but there was something else topping the Crimson Tide agenda at Bryant-Denny Stadium.

Alabama needed a confidence boost.

It seems odd to suggest that coming off the No. 1 vs. No. 3 showdown with Florida State, but it's true — especially with the offense. With two touchdowns, it had scored enough to defeat the Seminoles at Mercedes-Benz Stadium, but the 24-7 victory had been led by the defense and sparked by special teams.

"The big focus for our team was to improve, pay more attention to detail, play a little bit more disciplined as a team, and I think we probably accomplished that," Nick Saban said. "We did improve; we played better, especially on offense."

Overall, Alabama outgained Fresno State 497-274, including 305-58 on the ground. Sophomore quarterback Jalen Hurts ran for 154 yards, was 14-for-18 for 128 more in the air, and accounted for three touchdowns.

It was an impressive showing by the 19-year-old, but what Saban really noticed wasn't what he did, but how he did it.

Alabama's second possession was a good demonstration of his continuing development, especially the 23-yard touchdown throw to junior tight end Hale Hentges.

"Irv [Smith Jr.] and I were the primary targets," Hentges said of his first career touchdown. "It's a play that we've been running for a long time. For Jalen to look off [the safety] and hold him long enough until I'm open is a very veteran move."

That's what Alabama needed, especially with the young quarterback working with a new offensive coordinator, Brian Daboll. While fans clamored to see backup quarterback Tua Tagovailoa, they forgot that Hurts needed reps too.

"He had quite a few runs today that were very effective… and he was very efficient throwing the ball," Saban said. "I think the combination of those two things are going to make us better."

Running back Bo Scarbrough, who helped Alabama record 305 rushing yards, runs through the Fresno State defense.

PLAY OF THE GAME:

It's not very often that an offense's first rushing play results in a touchdown, but sophomore quarterback Jalen Hurts set the tone with his 55-yard zone-read option run.

So was getting more players involved in the passing game after junior Calvin Ridley was the only wide receiver to have a catch the week before. Alabama finished with 11 players having at least one reception.

It started spreading the ball around on the first play, a screen to senior wide receiver Cam Sims that resulted in an 18-yard gain, followed by a 55-yard zone-read option run by Hurts to give his team a 7-0 lead. The initial touchdown drive took just 39 seconds.

"We definitely wanted to come out fast," senior center Bradley Bozeman said.

It kept going. Alabama's subsequent two drives were more of the same, going 62 and 75 yards, as Hurts went over 4,000 total offensive yards for his career. His fourth possession also resulted in a touchdown, the drive going 77 yards and junior running back Damien Harris notching a 5-yard touchdown run.

In between the coaches inserted both Tagovailoa and true freshman right tackle Jedrick Wills Jr., if for no other reason for him to get their feet wet with the first-team offense.

Saban indicated that Alabama's plan all along was to get Tagovalioa into the game at some point of the second quarter. With no other veteran quarterbacks on the roster, the true freshman was the clear backup and didn't have a chance to play against Florida State — one of the few drawbacks to having such a flashy season opener.

There probably couldn't have haven a better time than when the Crimson Tide got the ball at the Bulldogs' 48 with a 21-3 lead.

Not surprisingly, his debut was sort of hit or miss. A 9-yard pass to senior wide receiver Robert Foster (his first catch of the season) was followed by a 6-yard throw

PLAYER OF THE GAME:

Hurts had 282 yards in total offense with 128 passing and 154 rushing, and three total touchdowns. Alabama averaged a 10.1-yard gain every time he didn't hand the ball off.

to Ridley. He then he took a bad sack and the drive quickly stalled. Despite the excellent field position, JK Scott came in for his first punt of the game.

"He'll obviously learn from it," Saban said. "We don't need to be taking negative plays."

Tagovailoa was re-inserted in the fourth quarter when both sides were trying to get players some valuable experience. Again, the results were mixed. Alabama moved the ball, but the first drive stalled at the Alabama 45 and the second at the Fresno State 4.

Things finally clicked on the Crimson Tide's final possession, a 75-yard drive on eight plays, capped by a 16-yard touchdown by freshman Henry Ruggs III. It was the first for both the quarterback and wide receiver.

It was a stepping stone for them, just like this game was for the Crimson Tide. The outcome was predictable as it notched the 66th straight win against an unranked opponent, and the offensive line still wasn't as imposing as the coaches wanted. But this was an important win in getting Alabama ready for the rest of the season.

Besides, Fresno State ended up playing for its conference title and ranked in the polls.

"I thought we did a way better job of executing," Hurts said. "The key to playing successful football is executing." ∎

Quarterback Jalen Hurts runs for one of his two first-half touchdowns in the 41-10 victory against Fresno State.

STAT OF THE GAME:

Hurts came very close to having more rushing yards on his first touchdown than Fresno State totaled in the game. The Bulldogs finished with 58, but had just 26 when Alabama pulled the first-team defense.

39

CORNERBACK
LEVI WALLACE
Former Walk-On Boosts Bama Defense

The radio show caller stumped the morning host, even though the Alabama campus was in the heart of the station's listening area. "Who is Levi Wallace?" the caller asked. "Where did he come from?"

Florida State fans probably had the same reaction after Wallace came off the bench to help settle the Crimson Tide defense during Alabama's 24-7 season-opening victory. The senior's third-quarter interception was when many of them knew for sure how the No. 1 vs. No. 3 showdown at Mercedes-Benz Stadium would turn out.

"I don't remember him going through recruiting or anything," the radio caller continued.

That's because he didn't. Wallace was a terrific high school athlete on the other side of the country, but he never had any Division I offers. He didn't plan on playing college football, content to just be a college student.

He's on the Crimson Tide because of his father, Walter, who hailed from Tuscaloosa and was a big Alabama fan.

Wallace walked on to the team in January of his freshman year, 2014.

Four months later, on the morning of the spring celebration known as A-Day, he found out his father had died from amyotrophic lateral sclerosis (ALS), otherwise known as Lou Gehrig's disease. Walter was 58.

Wallace still played, and has been playing for him ever since.

"I think about him all the time right before I go out onto the field, I look up and thank him for the opportunity, for believing in me," Wallace said.

"He's always on my mind."

Walter Wallace was married for 24 years and spent 21 years in the Air Force. He also started and developed numerous businesses in Tucson, Ariz., including Three Points Childcare and Preschool, and he coached the Arizona Titans Track Club.

He was close to his sons, Levi and Lawrence, and used to bring them on trips to Tuscaloosa.

"His dad was just a great guy," Tucson High Magnet School football coach Justin Argraves said. "He was always around, supporting Levi and Lawrence."

Levi was a two-way standout who never left the field for the Badgers, and that's not an exaggeration. He started at defensive back, going from corner to safety, played wide receiver on offense and was also the return man on special teams.

"Tremendous kid," the coach added. "When I met him first he was like 6-foot, lucky to weigh 150 pounds. Just a respectful young man. Did everything you asked."

Cornerback Levi Wallace readies to make a play during Alabama's 27-19 victory against Texas A&M, in which he had five tackles.

Due to his skinny frame, Wallace didn't get a sniff from any Division I programs, and got few looks even from smaller colleges. He wasn't in any recruiting databases, only appearing as a college player who was added in later on.

But the plan all along was for both brothers to attend Alabama, taking advantage of a GI Bill benefit for tuition. Even when Argraves took over the Tucson High Magnet School football program in 2011, Levi told him he would be attending Alabama, where he hoped to walk on. Younger brother Lawrence planned to join the track team.

Their father was diagnosed right before Levi left for Tuscaloosa and the fall 2013 semester.

"I had a lot going on in my life, so I was really ready to let football go," Wallace said. "My dad just kind of convinced me, 'Just see how good you are.' I wanted to see how it is going up against some of the best athletes, some of the best receivers that come to the University of Alabama. I just wanted to see how good I was.

"He just said he believed in me, he always believed in me and my abilities. He said, 'You're a great football player, so you might as well give it a shot and see where things go.'"

It took two years of working, learning, and developing; of coming back every day to measure up against those the university had already invested in, with no guarantees for tomorrow. Along the way, a former high school teammate was killed back in Arizona, adding to the grief he already felt for his father.

"It was real hard on Levi," Argraves said.

But during fall camp in 2016 Wallace was awarded a scholarship, as was his good friend linebacker Jamey Mosley. He subsequently saw his first game action in the season opener against Southern California, making his first collegiate tackle and notching his first broken pass.

Wallace played 11 games, became a special-teams staple and stepped in when cornerback Marlon Humphrey had to leave the Iron Bowl with a leg injury.

"He's one of the best technicians on the Alabama defense," defensive back Minkah Fitzpatrick said at the time. "That's why he's out there."

Wallace came into this season with 11 career tackles, two passes broken up, and a quarterback hurry, but he's been in the mix at left cornerback since the early parts of fall camp when Nick Saban called him "one of the guys that we're looking to create a role for." He soon started splitting reps with converted wide receiver Trevon Diggs on the first-team defense.

Diggs started and played the first two series against FSU, when the Seminoles had drives of eight and 11 yards while tallying 127 yards and seven points. On one play in front of the Alabama bench he got shoved back by a wide receiver and landed on his rear.

Wallace was inserted for the subsequent possession, and Florida State managed just 123 total yards the rest of the game.

He was credited with two tackles, but the play that made everyone ask, "Who's No. 39?" came on the first FSU snap following running back Damien Harris' 11-yard touchdown run. Wallace made the correct read and snared his first pickoff.

"He understands the system, understands and can make the adaptations," Saban said. "I think he was a little more comfortable in the game, being a big game, first game, all that. I think Trevon was a little nervous, a little anxious, made a couple of mistakes early. But I think it's important that both of those guys can play well for us."

So yes, with Mosley also getting time at strong-side linebacker, Alabama had two former walk-ons as part college football's most imposing defense over the previous decade, alongside the likes of Fitzpatrick, Da'Shawn Hand, Da'Ron Payne …

"Ever since I came in, I couldn't believe he was a walk-on," senior linebacker Shaun Dion Hamilton said about Wallace. "He's one of those under the radar guys and everybody inside the program knows how good he is. A guy who comes ready to work every day. I'm just glad he's on our team."

So was his dad, obviously. Plus, Wallace already has his business degree.

"I hope I made him proud," he said. ∎

Levi Wallace, who helped Alabama limit Clemson to 124 passing yards in the Sugar Bowl, tackles Tigers wide receiver Deon Cain.

ALABAMA 41, COLORADO STATE 23

SEPTEMBER 16, 2017 · TUSCALOOSA, ALABAMA

THE GOOD, THE BAD, AND THE UGLY

Bama Cruises to Easy Win Despite Defensive Struggles

"We're going to have a come-to-Jesus meeting on Monday," senior linebacker Shaun Dion Hamilton declared, which tells you exactly how Alabama felt about giving up 23 points to Colorado State.

It didn't matter that the Rams scored twice in the fourth quarter after Nick Saban had started inserting backups in hopes of getting them some valuable playing time. What irked the Crimson Tide was that after taking a 41-10 lead it seemed to stop trying to match CSU's intensity.

"We didn't execute very well defensively: not stopping the run; not getting off field on the third down; didn't play great in the red zone," Saban said. "We have a lot of work to do. We made a lot of mental errors with the new guys playing, in some cases different positions. The continuity and togetherness is not what it needs to be on that side of the ball.

"They made some plays that I wasn't pleased with."

When the Crimson Tide goes over the game film each week, Saban has a segment named after the famous 1966 movie "The Good, the Bad, and the Ugly," featuring plays that demonstrate each. He's going to have plenty to talk about with all three categories.

For the good, the defense gave up just 11 total yards in the first quarter, made two turnovers that led to points including senior safety Hootie Jones' first career interception, and broke up nine passes, four by senior cornerback Levi Wallace in his second start.

The bad will include giving up 391 total yards and CSU scoring on all four trips to the red zone.

As for the ugly, Colorado State was 10 of 17 on third downs and had a time of possession advantage of 33:53-26:07. The Rams had four possessions of double-digit plays and scored on all of them — 12, 11, 11, and 15, accounting for 297 yards.

"There were some third-down situations, third-and-12 and third-and-13 that you've got to get off the field in those situations," Saban said. "(Colorado State) made plays that we normally would make that we didn't make, and that allowed them to keep the ball. We busted a coverage and gave them a 50-yard play where the corner fired and nobody covered his guy.

"We didn't execute, that's what happened. We didn't execute."

The real question is why Alabama didn't execute like it had hoped, and while it's difficult for a team to keep its edge when up 41-10 and the stands are empting, one position group in particular struggled.

Quarterback Jalen Hurts signals to his team during the victory against Colorado State, in which he accounted for 351 total yards.

PLAY OF THE GAME:

Senior wide receiver Robert Foster's 52-yard touchdown just before halftime capped a 2-minute drive and helped Alabama reclaim the momentum.

It shouldn't come as a surprise to anyone which one it was: the linebackers.

Colorado State was well aware of Alabama's injury issues and tried to take full advantage. It ran a lot of I-formation plays and with a veteran quarterback leading an experienced group of supporting players targeted the replacements in the passing game.

With junior Christian Miller (bicep) and sophomore Terrell Lewis (elbow) likely to miss the rest of the season, and fellow outside linebacker Anferee Jennings (ankle) sidelined along with senior interior linebacker Rashaan Evans (groin), Alabama thought it could be okay if it didn't suffer any more setbacks.

But true freshman Dylan Moses (undisclosed) wasn't available this week and junior interior linebacker Keith Holcombe spent quite a bit of time in the medical tent with what looked like an ankle injury. He returned and led all tacklers with nine, but the Crimson Tide was dangerously thin at the position.

"We have five linebackers who aren't playing," Saban said. "I don't care who you are, what team you are, that creates some issues and some problems."

There's no better example than what Penn State went through in 2016.

The Nittany Lions lost middle linebacker Jason Cabinda in the opener, and then their best outside linebacker Brandon Bell a week later. Nyeem Wartman-White subsequently joined them, suffering a season-ending knee injury for the second-straight year.

During that stretch, Penn State lost to Pitt 42-39, survived Temple 34-27, and without three starting linebackers was crushed at No. 4 Michigan, 49-10. Penn State was down to using former walk-ons and inexperienced players.

Sound familiar?

PLAYER OF THE GAME:

Sophomore quarterback Jalen Hurts' 232.0 passer-efficiency rating was a career best. He was 12 for 17 for 248 yards and two passing touchdowns, with 11 carries for 103 rushing yards and another score without having any turnovers.

Cabinda and Bell returned for the upset win against Ohio State in mid-October, when with Manny Bowen they combined to make 43 tackles and two sacks. Penn State didn't lose again until the Rose Bowl after barely missing the College Football Playoff.

Alabama's only starting linebacker playing against Colorado State was Hamilton, who was coming off an ACL injury suffered in the SEC Championship Game. Holcombe and former walk-on Jamey Mosley made their second straight starts while true freshman Christopher Allen was more in the mix at the other outside spot.

"All these guys are scholarship guys …" said Hamilton, banging the no-excuse drum that started to be heard as Alabama turned its attention to its SEC opener at Vanderbilt, which would be coming off a big win against No. 18 Kansas State.

The good news for Alabama was that Evans appeared to be close to returning. He was in uniform, but didn't warm up against the Rams. Jennings probably wasn't too far behind. Even so, there was going to be some barking by Alabama's defensive leaders, who Saban likes to call the alpha dogs.

"We were on the field entirely too long," Hamilton said. "All it takes is one person not to do his job and a play is made, just like that. We have to execute. We have to play better." ■

Quarterback Jalen Hurts runs through the Colorado State defense for part of his game-high 103 rushing yards.

STAT OF THE GAME:

Excluding when Alabama had been trying to run out the clock at the end of a half, Hurts was on the field for 28 possessions. The Crimson Tide scored on 17 of them with three missed field goals and eight punts.

ALABAMA 59, VANDERBILT 0

SEPTEMBER 23, 2017 · NASHVILLE, TENNESSEE

DOMINATION

Bama Silences Vandy, Pitches Shutout

What else could anyone say, except maybe "oops."

Seven days previous, the moment got to Vanderbilt senior defensive lineman Nifae Lealao a little too much. After the Commodores pulled off an upset over visiting No. 18 Kansas State, he said the wrong thing during a brief postgame interview on the field.

"We expected to get this," he said. "When you come to our house we show you how to play some SEC ball.

"Alabama, you're next."

As some people say before initiating a beat down, "Them's fightin' words," or at last that's the way the Crimson Tide took it. It simply crushed the Commodores to open league play, 59-0.

Led by junior running back Damien Harris, who had a career-best 151 yards on 12 carries and three touchdowns, the Crimson Tide tallied 496 rushing yards, the most by Alabama during the Nick Saban era. Alabama notched six rushing touchdowns, two receiving scores, and a field goal.

Meanwhile, the defense limited the Commodores to 78 total yards of offense, 40 rushing and 38 passing. Not only did that set a new Alabama standard under Saban, but the three first downs allowed were the fewest by an SEC team in 20 years.

Vanderbilt converted just one third-down opportunity and the best field position at the end of a possession was at its own 44, the first drive that concluded with an interception.

"At Alabama, we want to be respected, and we don't feel like they were showing us respect," Jalen Hurts said. "So, we came out here and tried to play Alabama football."

The sophomore quarterback who was 9-for-17 for 78 yards and ran for 48 more before taking an early seat added that the instructions from the coaching staff were simple, "To dominate."

Here's the very definition of that: Alabama's possession chart had punt, four straight touchdowns (drives of five, two, six and 13 plays, respectively), punt, field goal, four straight touchdowns (eight, eight, four and 10), and it ran out the clock with a 15-play possession to eat up the last 11:45.

Both coaches said afterward that the Crimson Tide getting off to a good start was the key, with Derek Mason adding the line that countless opposing coaches had previously used, "There's a reason why they're No. 1."

Defensive lineman Da'Shawn Hand celebrates a fumble recovery, one of two turnovers that Alabama forced against Vanderbilt.

PLAY OF THE GAME:

With Alabama ahead 7-0 late in the first quarter, the 61-yard touchdown on a cutback run by junior running back Damien Harris sparked the rout.

"Credit Alabama," he said. "Alabama is exactly what we thought they were going into the game. They're great defensively, they're well-coached, and they're physical. We got in a hole early and it snowballed on us. We struggled offensively and defensively on third downs. We struggled to get third downs on offense and struggled to get off the field on third downs on defense.

"We were out-coached. We looked like a tired team at the end. We got out-classed."

With the win, Alabama notched its 19th consecutive win against SEC Eastern Division opponents, dating back to a 35-21 loss at No. 19 South Carolina in 2010. It included four wins in the SEC Championship Game. It also extended the program's string of wins against an unranked opponent to 68, and was Saban's 54th career game coaching Alabama when it was ranked No. 1 in the Associated Press Top 25.

It also did so while using numerous reserves. Playing exclusively in the second half, freshman quarterback Tua Tagovailoa was 8-for-10 for 103 yards and two touchdowns, to freshmen wide receivers Jerry Jeudy and Devonta Smith.

In addition to Harris' three rushing touchdowns, junior running back Bo Scarbrough had two and true freshman running back Brian Robinson Jr. had one while averaging 10.2 yards per carry. Overall, Alabama's ground game gained 7.5 yards per attempt.

Meanwhile, the Crimson Tide defense was arguably even better.

Vanderbilt starting quarterback Kyle Shurmer completed four passes out of 20 attempts, and nothing longer than 8 yards. The longest running play went for 9 yards. The Commodores executed just 38 plays, compared to 93 for the visiting team, and averaged 2.1 yards per snap.

PLAYER OF THE GAME:

Harris had 151 rushing yards on 12 carries and scored three touchdowns to pace the Crimson Tide.

Senior linebacker Shaun Dion Hamilton led the defense with five tackles, while no one else took more than three. Linebacker Anfernee Jennings forced a fumble that was recovered by defensive lineman Da'Shawn Hand. Junior safety Ronnie Harrison had the interception and the Crimson Tide broke up six passes.

"All we wanted to do was to play with passion to show how much we love this game," said senior linebacker Rashaan Evans after returning from a painful groin injury (that was still healing). "I feel like we did that today and we want to continue to do that throughout the year." ∎

Running back Damien Harris scores one of his three rushing touchdowns in the 59-0 victory against Vanderbilt.

STAT OF THE GAME:

Alabama outgained Vanderbilt in total offense 677-78, and set a school record with 38 first downs.

ALABAMA 66, OLE MISS 3

SEPTEMBER 30, 2017 · TUSCALOOSA, ALABAMA

RESOUNDING ANSWER

Alabama Destroys Ole Miss in Record-Setting Performance

There's an old phrase, which might date back to the ancient Greeks, about how an elephant never forgets.

Well, neither does Nick Saban.

It's the only conclusion one can draw after Alabama completely destroyed Ole Miss.

The Crimson Tide still remembered the back-to-back losses to the Rebels, 23-17 and 43-37 in 2014 and 2015, respectively. The memory of fans storming the field at Vaught–Hemingway Stadium in one, and the crazy bounces in the other were still fresh, along with falling behind 24-3 last year.

Saban had warned everyone by saying that the ultimate disrespect is when "someone quietly thinks they have your number."

This was Alabama's answer: 66-3.

"They came to our house and Coach Saban said we had to defeat somebody and not just win the game," junior All-American defensive back Minkah Fitzpatrick said. "I think we did a good job of defeating them, demoralizing them, and just playing our game."

For three quarters, Alabama absolutely annihilated the Rebels. It looked like it wanted to go for extinction until Saban finally pulled back with the reserves in the fourth quarter.

Still, the results were impressive. Alabama's 66 points were the most ever scored by a Saban-coached team, and the Crimson Tide crushed its first two SEC opponents on the schedule by a combined 125-3.

It's the first time Alabama scored more than 50 points in consecutive SEC games since defeating Kentucky, 60-19, and Vanderbilt, 71-0, on Nov. 3 and Nov. 17, 1945 — and teams were very hit-or-miss during World War II when a lot of schools didn't play football.

It also did so with both the offense and defense feeling like they haven't come close to peaking yet.

Alabama's offense had 613 total yards and still felt it left a lot out on the field.

The defense had 10 tackles for a loss including five sacks, and didn't allow a third-down conversion in 13 attempts. Yet on a scale of one to 10 senior linebacker Rashaan Evans still scored their performance a "five."

He was serious, but in fairness he was still upset about the knee injury to senior defensive end Da'Shawn Hand, which turned out to be an MCL sprain that would sideline him for the rest of the month.

"It was really kind of sad. He's a big part of our defense," Evans said. "For anybody to go down like that it was devastating. Hopefully his injury is not that bad."

"He's a guy that we definitely need."

Tight end Hale Hentges celebrates his touchdown catch, which gave Alabama a 21-0 lead.

PLAY OF THE GAME:

Even though it occurred just 5 minutes into the game, senior cornerback Levi Wallace's interception return for a touchdown made it clear to everyone watching how the game would turn out.

Alabama's SEC schedule will only get harder, but neither big win should be overlooked. After defeating then-No. 18 Kansas State at home, Vanderbilt probably should have been ranked in the polls.

Ole Miss wasn't the same with NCAA sanctions looming and without Hugh Freeze, who had been fired right after SEC media days in July. Nevertheless, the 66 points scored were the most ever by either team in the series that dated back to 1894.

That's when the "Golden Age" of piracy was at its peak, which was sort of fitting as a reference because Alabama was simply taking no prisoners.

Consider the defensive play-call when Ole Miss had third-and-6 at the Alabama 39 early in the second quarter, and the Crimson Tide was already ahead 28-3. Coordinator Jeremy Pruitt went for the throat by blitzing Fitzpatrick, who dropped Shea Patterson for a 12-yard sack before the quarterback realized he was toast.

Or the offense suddenly unveiling the two-back set for the first time this season, with sophomore Josh Jacobs the beneficiary.

But even more telling was Alabama hiring former Ole Miss offensive coordinator Dan Werner in March. Two years ago, with Werner helping direct the offense, Ole Miss set program records for scoring (531), touchdowns (68), total offense (6,731), passing yards (4,351), passing touchdowns (35), 50-plus point games (four), and games with more than 600 yards of offense (three).

The Rebels also led the SEC and were top 10 nationally in scoring (40.8), total offense (517.8 yards per game), and passing (334.7).

He helped Alabama create a potent offense, and it sure couldn't have hurt the defense to have him around prior to this specific game.

Part of an effort that limited Ole Miss to 88 rushing yards, Alabama freshman defensive lineman Quinnen Williams tackles running back Eric Swinney.

PLAYER OF THE GAME:

Sophomore quarterback Jalen Hurts was 12-for-19 for 197 yards and two touchdowns in the passing game, and had 101 rushing yards on 10 attempts for another touchdown before being pulled in the third quarter. During one stretch he had nine straight completions, which accounted for all but 16 of his passing yards.

Thus, the strong message that Alabama sent at the close of September: We're not messing around.

Fans had been looking for an identity with this team, and in terms of Xs and Os that would continue to develop as the season progressed. But in terms of results, no one was complaining. Excluding when Alabama was running out the clock at the end of a half, it had scored on 32 of its 43 offensive possessions over the past four games, or 74.4 percent. The other 11 ended with two missed field goals and nine punts by JK Scott. The offense had yet to lose a turnover.

As for the team's mindset, the Crimson Tide was playing like it was angry for not winning the national championship the previous season, and focused one thing: payback on a grand scale.

"Our goal as a team is to go out there and dominate," Hurts said. "That's just what we want to do. We just have to do it consistently." ■

STAT OF THE GAME:

Nine different players scored touchdowns for Alabama while Ole Miss had nine receivers or running backs touch the ball. Not one of them reached the end zone.

MOST POINTS SCORED BY SABAN-COACHED TEAMS

66-3, Ole Miss at Alabama, Sept. 30, 2017
63-7, Georgia State at Alabama, Nov. 18, 2010
62-13, Alabama at Duke, Sept. 18, 2010
59-0, Alabama at Vanderbilt, Sept. 23, 2017
59-0, Texas A&M at Alabama, Oct. 18, 2014
59-13, LSU at Arizona, Sept. 6, 2003

5

RUNNING BACK
RONNIE CLARK

Clark's First Score Was Worth More Than Six Points

Sometimes in football, a touchdown is not just a touchdown.

That was the case with Alabama's final score against Ole Miss, which prompted such an emotional celebration on the Crimson Tide sideline that even Nick Saban had to admit it probably should have drawn a penalty.

Even so, it would have been worth it, because everyone who was overly exuberant about Ronnie Clark's first career touchdown knew the full story. It was about a lot more than an athlete coming back from major injuries; it was about seeing someone overcome so much that you couldn't help but root for him.

So, yes, the touchdown was special, as was the reaction of his teammates. Nearly a week later, Clark still wasn't sure which meant more to him.

"They're both about the same, because I hadn't scored a touchdown since high school, because of all the stuff that I've been through," Clark said. "It was just kind of shocking to me. I was amazed at the same time, but I was happy that I had got it done."

The on-field reaction was just the beginning. Friends and teammates spoke proudly and took to social media, like one of his former high school assistant coaches posting that Clark had been scoring touchdowns on and off the field "for a really long time."

"Ronnie's one of those dudes that he cares about everyone, like everybody," sophomore running back Josh Jacobs said.

"We all love Ronnie Clark to death," junior tight end Hale Hentges said.

Saban referred to him as the "consummate, ultimate great story about any program and what college football should be all about."

What most Crimson Tide fans knew about Clark were his prolific high school years before signing with Alabama, and the injuries he had since endured.

In 2013-14, Clark was considered one of the top five recruits in the state after a stellar career at Calera High School that resulted in invitations to play in both the Alabama-Mississippi All-State Game and the Under Armour All-America Game.

His high school career had actually gotten off to an early start in eighth grade, when Coach Wiley McKeller made Clark a slot receiver because he was already better at the position than anyone else on the roster. Three

Running back Ronnie Clark warms up before the Sugar Bowl in New Orleans, where Alabama triumphed over Clemson.

years later, the coach moved him to quarterback because he was already the leader of the offense, while also playing him on defense.

Clark never complained about all the different roles. As a high school senior, he completed about 70 percent of his passes and accounted for more than 2,500 yards and 35 touchdowns, while leading the Eagles into the state playoffs.

"He is an ace of a guy," said McKeller, now the coach at Vincent High School. "I've had the luck to coach some really good athletes, but the way he carries himself and his demeanor and work ethic is what really sets him apart. He's the standard by which I judge all other kids with above-average ability now. I can't help it, it just pops in my head, like 'Ronnie Clark was never late to a practice,' or 'Ronnie Clark was never tardy to a class.'

"You see so many guys that do have a sense of entitlement because they might be a little bit bigger or a little bit faster in high school, and here's a guy who's just completely selfless. Tremendous leader, tremendous guy."

Alabama's coaches were initially thinking defensive back with Clark, but ended up placing him with the running backs. He redshirted in 2014 and played three games during the subsequent season when during the individual drills of a practice gave a burst, felt a pop and went down in a heap. His left Achilles had torn, the first major injury Clark had ever experienced.

Naturally, he was heartbroken.

"Definitely," he said. "The Achilles is how you walk, you know what I'm saying? It's a thing that you need because you walk every day. It was kind of a struggle at first."

An Achilles tear is more common in sports like basketball and gymnastics, but there are some certainties about the recovery process: It takes a long time, often a full year until an athlete can compete again, and they're often unable to do so at the same level.

"You pretty much have to learn how to run again,

learn how to walk again," Clark said. "Once you tear it you're not walking for a couple of months and then once you start back walking it's a process. It's a long, nagging process and it's a tough one to come back from too."

Clark did come back only to have the same thing happen on the right side, this time while working with the punt team. It was near the end of the Crimson Tide's final spring practice, and he didn't even need the trainers to tell him what had happened.

"I tore it the same way, just taking off to run," he said. "It felt the exact same as the left one felt."

Some people would have said that's it, enough is enough, if not with the first setback the second. No one would have blamed Clark if he had bowed out gracefully and said, "Well, I gave it a shot."

He says he never considered quitting.

"I've always been a competitor, and I've always wanted to complete and play football, that's what I love to do," Clark said. "The love I have for the game, the passion I have for it, I never thought about it through the injuries and everything."

The everything he alluded to serves as his inspiration, motivation, and sounding board: his mother.

Kimberly Clark has muscular dystrophy, which is a group of disorders that leads to progressive loss of muscle mass and loss of strength. When she watches her son play for the Crimson Tide it's from a wheelchair.

"I think about her," Clark said about putting his injuries into perspective. "There's nothing that compares to what she's going through."

Not only did she need assistance with day-to-day things that most people take for granted, like walking, washing, and dressing, but so did Clark's grandmother, who moved in with the family while dealing with a brain tumor.

With his father's job for a railroad company frequently taking him out of town, Clark had to do a lot of things that most of his high school peers

Alabama's Brandon Kennedy and Derek Kief celebrate with Ronnie Clark following Clark's first touchdown of his college career.

couldn't begin to fathom.

"I started at about 13-14," he said about helping his mother and grandmother. "It kind of matured me into the young man I am today. It made me see a lot more than what the average teenager sees.

"It taught me a lot."

Like patience, perseverance, and not being afraid to step up or speak out when necessary. Yet the experiences didn't alter who he was at the core, and they only intensified his ability to lead. For example, when first asked about the touchdown, Clark's initial response was: "I'm not an individual type of guy, I'm a team guy. I

scored this for my team."

With his latest comeback, Clark spent time working at tight end but he was soon back as a full-time running back. He nearly scored during the final minutes at Vanderbilt, but fully understood why the coaches opted to take a knee at 59-0.

He didn't have to wait long for opportunity to come around again, a 9-yard run with 6:51 to go to cap Alabama's 66-3 victory against Rebels.

For those who have stood by Clark all these years, the score was irrelevant. You bet they were celebrating.

"It felt good," Clark said. "It was unbelievable." ∎

JUST GOOD ENOUGH

Bama Withstands Late A&M Rally and Stays Perfect

This time, Gene Stallings could have all the hugs he wanted, but there would be none at midfield.

Fifty years after the protégé bested the master, with Paul "Bear" Bryant famously embracing his former assistant at the Cotton Bowl, the former Alabama and Texas A&M coach especially known for strong defensive play saw the Crimson Tide do just enough against the Aggies.

Alabama gave up its first touchdowns against an SEC opponent, ending a streak during which it scored 149 points while yielding just six. It also shut down the Aggies' running game and created three turnovers en route to a 27-19 victory.

"We made some huge defensive stops or this game could have turned out differently," a frustrated Nick Saban said afterward.

No. 1 Alabama won in front of Stallings, who eight days following a heart attack saluted the crowd at Kyle Field as Texas A&M celebrated the anniversary of his 1967 team, but it was anything but a perfect performance.

Thanks to a couple of clutch plays, including a diving 2-yard touchdown catch by Christian Kirk that probably should have been reviewed, the Aggies passed for 237 yards and had a time-of-possession advantage of 32:28–27:32.

They also were able to come back from a 24-3 deficit and get the crowd of 101,058 back into the game for the final minutes, the real cause of Saban's angst (that resulted in his popular quote: "I'm trying to get our players to listen to me instead of listening to you guys. All that stuff you write about how good we are, all that stuff they hear on ESPN, it's like poison. It's like taking poison. Like rat poison.")

"We didn't finish the game," he said. "That's not how good teams play."

But it could have been worse. Texas A&M had a red-zone drive snuffed out by a Minkah Fitzpatrick interception at the Alabama 1, on third-and-5. Texas A&M was still about to turn it into points as the subsequent possession resulted in a blocked punt for a safety, and a touchdown off blown coverage with defensive back Tony Brown out with a sprained knee, only to see Fitzpatrick recover the onside kick.

"The interception was big," Saban said, but added about Fitzpatrick's onside-kick return: "He actually should have went down. The only way you can lose the game is if he fumbles the ball. He knows that, he'll learn."

Texas A&M's Kellen Mond is hit by Alabama's Anfernee Jennings as he attempts to throw a pass during the second quarter. Mond's pass was incomplete, and Alabama would go on to record its sixth win.

PLAY OF THE GAME:

Although junior running back Damien Harris' 27-yard run to set up Alabama's second touchdown was in some ways more impressive, his 75-yard touchdown carry answered Texas A&M's early field goal just 13 seconds later.

PLAYER OF THE GAME:

Alabama's most consistent player on defense was junior defensive back Minkah Fitzpatrick, who was credited with five tackles including two for a loss, one forced fumble, an interception at the Alabama 1, and broke up a pass.

So will the defensive line, which was without senior defensive end Da'Shawn Hand (sprained knee). Instead, junior Isaiah Buggs led the Crimson Tide with a career-high 10 tackles (six solo and some featuring very hard hits), and sophomore Raekwon Davis tallied eight stops, a sack, and a fumble recovery that landed him the team's turnover belt for the first time.

He held it up like a wrestling champion.

"He's always excited when he makes a big play," said junior defensive tackle Da'Ron Payne, who was credited with six tackles.

But more than once Aggies freshman quarterback Kellen Mond was able to escape Alabama's pass rush and make something happen downfield. That included the 39-yard bomb to freshman wide receiver Camron Buckley in the final moments, setting up the touchdown to make it a one-score game.

Senior linebacker Rashaan Evans had Alabama's other fumble recovery while the defense gave up just 71 rushing yards and only one carry longer than 10 yards, a 20-yard run by Mond.

"We just really emphasized getting the ball out," Evans said.

Also on the plus side, after Texas A&M opened the scoring with a 52-yard field goal, the next seven Aggies possessions went: punt, fumble, punt, punt, fumble, fumble, downs — which went from 9:46 left in the first quarter, to 1:39 remaining in the third quarter.

Only in between the Crimson Tide didn't put the game away.

"We didn't do our best, but we got the win," Payne said. ∎

Alabama's Raekwon Davis (left) celebrates with Rashaan Evans after recovering a fumble.

Running back Damien Harris eludes Texas A&M's Larry Pryor as he rushes for an Alabama first down.

ALABAMA 41, ARKANSAS 9

OCTOBER 14, 2017 · TUSCALOOSA, ALABAMA

KEEP ON ROLLING

Crimson Tide Looks Sharp Against Razorbacks

Alabama sophomore quarterback Jalen Hurts couldn't help himself when arriving in the postgame interview room, where Damien Harris was still at the podium.

"Hi Damien," he loudly said in the middle of Harris giving an answer, perhaps the first thing that had successfully broken his concentration all night long. Hurts then chimed in with a question with his own, asking the junior running back to describe the Crimson Tide's first play from a scrimmage, a 75-yard cutback touchdown to kick-start Alabama's 41-9 victory at Bryant-Denny Stadium.

"I already answered that," Harris said with a smile.

"Yeah, but now I'm asking you," was the quick retort.

So Harris told it again: "We were trying to get the edge on an outside zone play. The entire defense sort of flew across the field. We knew going into this game that if they overran the play that we'd be able to cut back and maybe have an explosive play."

For the most part, Alabama seemed to have all the answers on this Saturday, with Harris running for 125 yards on nine carries and two touchdowns—the second effort from 4 yards out being much tougher than his first.

The offense tallied 496 total yards including 308 rushing, while the defense returned to its smothering ways.

The Crimson Tide notched five sacks and nine tackles for a loss, to go with 11 hurries and six passes broken up, while the Razorbacks averaged under a yard per carry (27 yards on 29 attempts). The only touchdown Alabama allowed came against the defensive reserves.

With Razorbacks starting quarterback Austin Allen out, Arkansas turned to Cole Kelley, the six-foot-seven reserve with a tight end body, but a bit of a gun-slinging arm. Of all the players who took to the field, he ended up with the dirtiest uniform of anyone by far, just the way the Crimson Tide had hoped.

"I felt like if we could just rattle that guy, he's obviously one of the biggest quarterback that we've faced," senior linebacker Rashaan Evans said.

"It was very difficult (to bring him down)."

But Alabama did, time and time again, and at one point Arkansas had just 37 yards of total offense when Kelley connected with Jordan Jones for a 46-yard completion just before halftime. Already down 24-0, Razorbacks coach Bret Bielema decided to go for a last-second touchdown from the 3-yard line only to have Crimson Tide safety Ronnie Harrison intercede.

It might have been the most telling point of the game for Nick Saban.

Defensive back Hootie Jones (left) and linebacker Mack Wilson are elated after Wilson intercepted a pass against Arkansas.

PLAY OF THE GAME:

While his 75-yard touchdown run on the first snap set the tone, the 4-yard score by junior running back Damien Harris was more impressive. Arkansas nickel back Kevin Richardson had him lined up for a 6-yard loss, but Harris got past him, avoided safety Josh Liddell's tackle and took a full-on hit from safety Santos Ramirez before plowing through defensive end T.J. Smith to reach the end zone.

73

Coming in, the coach had challenged his team following the "rat poison" game the previous week — not liking the way Alabama had let Texas A&M pull close enough that it had to recover an onside kick during the final seconds.

That the defense didn't yield even after the long pass gave him a strong indication of how his team would likely play the second half. Most of his starters were on the sideline early in the fourth quarter.

"I think we learned a lot of lessons in the Texas A&M game," Saabn said. "I think we gradually responded. I didn't know how the team was going to play today, to be honest with you; I didn't know how exactly we would do it.

"I think we had a little better week of practice, and I was pleased with their effort today. We did prepare a little bit better for this game."

Of course, it wasn't a perfect game, even if Arkansas was using a backup quarterback. Three fumbles on punt returns obviously stuck out, and the Crimson Tide's passing game could have been better. Hurts finished 12-for-19 for 155 yards and one touchdown, with eight different players making a reception, but he also had his first interception of the season.

The second longest streak in school history (ironically with record holder AJ McCarron looking on as the Cincinnati Bengals were on a bye) ended at 206 attempts. Hurts' previous pickoff had been in the second quarter against Auburn game on Nov. 24, 2016.

Yet with the win, Alabama (7-0, 4-0 SEC) felt like it was back on the right track.

"We knew we had to pick it up," senior center Bradley Bozeman said.

"I felt like the team responded very well," Evans said. "We sort of wanted to redeem ourselves, as far as how we played in the third and fourth quarters. That

PLAYER OF THE GAME:
Senior linebacker Rashaan Evans is beginning to get past the nasty groin injury suffered in the season opener. He was credited with six tackles including 3.5 for a loss and two sacks, and had a forced fumble and three quarterback hurries as the first-team defense yielded just three points. He gets bonus points for the sumo-style bow after one of his sacks.

was really the main focus and I feel like we did a really good job with that."

As for Harris, he got a little banged up, but notched his third 100-yard rushing game out of the last four, and eventually left the podium feeling pretty good about both himself and the team's direction.

"I heard Coach Saban say that he thought we did a good job," Harris said. "If he said that, I'm not going to disagree with him." ■

Head Coach Nick Saban was pleased with his team's performance against Arkansas, an improvement over the previous week's win against Texas A&M.

STAT OF THE GAME:
Arkansas had just three plays that were longer than Harris' average of 13.9 yards per rushing attempt.

ALABAMA 45, TENNESSEE 7
OCTOBER 21, 2017 · TUSCALOOSA, ALABAMA

LIGHT 'EM UP
Alabama Never Loses Fire in Rout of Tennessee

You would have thought the game was on the line. The crowd was certainly into it, and the defense was playing like it was mad. Despite being ahead by 31 points in the fourth quarter, with the smell of celebratory cigar smoke already overpowering Bryant-Denny stadium, Alabama wasn't ready to concede anything more on the scoreboard, not even a meaningless touchdown. Another botched punt return had given Tennessee the ball in the red zone, and the subsequent third-and-goal from the 1 brought back some unfavorable memories from the end of the previous season.

"We basically went back to Clemson and we wanted to stop them on the goal-line," senior linebacker Rashaan Evans said. "We wanted to do a great job of finishing."

They did. With a false-start penalty backing the Volunteers up and a fourth-down desperation pass over the middle intercepted by sophomore Mack Wilson, the defense made its stand to cap a 45-7 victory.

It was exactly what Nick Saban had wanted to see—along with the haze that soon covered a campus that's otherwise smoke-free the other 364 days of the year.

"That probably speaks a lot to what this game means and what this rivalry is," Saban said of the goal-line stand. "There was lot of pride going on out there."

Now he just needs to get the offense to match that intensity.

As expected, Alabama easily won the Third Saturday in October rivalry game for the 11th straight year, but the overall performance reflected just where this team is eight games into the season.

Overall, the No. 1 Crimson Tide outgained the Volunteers 604-108, averaging 7.0 yards per play compared to 2.3 allowed (10.1 and 2.8 in the air, respectively). The Alabama defense tallied nine tackles for a loss including four sacks and eight quarterback hurries, while Tennessee converted just one third-down opportunity.

Coming in, Tennessee running back John Kelly lead the SEC in all-purpose yards and yards from scrimmage (133.7). He was limited to 63 rushing yards, 18 on a blown draw play, and five receiving. The Vols' longest passing play was for just 12 yards as quarterback Jarrett Guarantano took numerous hard hits.

"You could see that we were doing everything we could to get him to scramble, or throw a bad pass," Evans said.

Having given up just 31 points in five SEC games, the defense looked like it was ready to match up against

Alabama's Damien Harris celebrates his first-half touchdown in front of the home crowd at Bryant-Denny.

PLAY OF THE GAME:
Sophomore linebacker Mack Wilson's interception on fourth-and-goal at the 5-yard-line kept Tennessee's offense from scoring a single point. Credited with pressuring the quarterback on the play were linebackers Rashaan Evans and Anfernee Jennings, who both came back from significant injuries suffered in the season opener.

PLAYER OF THE GAME:

Senior cornerback Levi Wallace was credited with six tackles, including three for a loss, two sacks, and a quarterback hurry. Overall, Tennessee's longest reception was just 12 yards, and the only two significant running plays were both draws.

anyone. At least it did on paper. Alabama was facing its third straight freshman quarterback.

Meanwhile, Tennessee's passing defense topped the SEC by yielding just 129.2 yards per game, but the Vols' rushing defense was the league's worst.

Alabama still ran for 272 yards and passed for 332, but wasn't satisfied with its performance. Even sophomore quarterback Jalen Hurts called the offense "sloppy" and "sluggish" during a very odd first half.

After Alabama went 63 yards on 12 plays on its opening possession, the passing game fell out of sync, including during one of the most bizarre possessions of the season.

Up 7-0, Alabama had second-and-13 at the Tennessee 43 when Hurts found an open Irv Smith across the middle, only to have the sophomore tight end fumble through the end zone for an apparent touchback.

Only it wasn't. Defensive end Jonathan Kongbo, who hadn't lived up to his billing as a top junior-college prospect, was called for a blatant personal foul for hands to the face that not only nullified the fumble (if the defense commits a penalty at any point up until it has possession then the ball stays with the offense), but gave Alabama the first down at the 2-yard line.

Two penalties and numerous plays later, Alabama scored the exact same way as its initial drive, inserting defensive lineman Da'Ron Payne as a fullback and calling for junior running back Bo Scarbrough over the top from the 1.

With fans on both sides confused from the odd sequence, Alabama had a 14-0 lead following the 15-play, 85-yard touchdown drive and then quickly scored again (with Kongo committing the same infraction against Crimson Tide left tackle Jonah Williams) to take a commanding 21-0 halftime lead.

Running back Bo Scarbrough soars above Tennessee's defense on his way to the end zone.

STAT OF THE GAME:
At one point late in the third quarter, Alabama's offense had run nearly as many plays, 70, as Tennessee had in total yards, 74. The Crimson Tide would have finished with 500 more total yards (604-108), but lost four when twice taking a knee to run out the clock. Also, UT had more punts (nine) than first downs (seven).

"The whole idea was to come there with intensity, do our jobs and do it with some fire in our eyes," said Hurts, who finished 13-for-21 for 198 yards, one touchdown and no turnovers.

When he led a precise up-tempo drive for another touchdown to open the second half, Saban had seen enough and pulled him in favor of Tua Tagovailoa.

The left-hander completed his first four passes and had Alabama knocking on the door for another score when the true freshman made a mistake over the middle, with linebacker Daniel Bituli returning the interception 97-yards to score the Volunteers' first touchdown since facing UMass on Sept. 23.

"Tua had that same face that I had," said Hurts, comparing it to his fumble on his very first play against Southern California in 2016. "That's a good thing."

Regardless, while Tennessee's offense didn't score again, the Crimson Tide offense was left kicking itself due to inconsistency. The difference demonstrated just how far apart these programs have become, in addition to the Alabama players saying they were already telling themselves before halftime what Saban said in the locker room during the break, that they had to play better.

"To be honest I think we're probably playing at a five or a six," Scarbrough said about offense's execution on a scale of 10. "We can be way better than we are right now." ■

Quarterback Tua Tagovailoa pushes past Tennessee defensive back Theo Jackson for a touchdown, capping a 23-yard run.

NEED FOR SPEED
Alabama's Running Game is Key to Success

Damien Harris couldn't help himself. The junior running back was going past the Alabama football team's media room while Josh Jacobs was being interviewed, and he popped in just in time to hear the question: "Can you throw the ball as well?"

"No, he can't," Harris bellowed from behind the row of cameras. "No, he can't. No, he can't. I'm here to tell you all he can't throw the ball."

And just for good measure, he added another: "No. He can't."

Alas, someone seems to have finally found something that a Crimson Tide running back can't do on the field this season, although it should be noted that Jacobs did play some quarterback in high school. He was more of a wildcat-style quarterback at Tulsa (Okla.) McLain, but he still completed some passes.

"When you haven't thrown a ball in a year and a half …" Jacobs said.

Harris offered a final "No" while heading for the door, but at this point no one should rule anything out when it comes to the Crimson Tide backfield.

There's talent, depth and versatility, plus a line that's started to really come together, making the running game the biggest strength of the offense. The No. 1 Crimson Tide took full advantage with 2,118 rushing yards through the first seven games.

The average of 302.6 yards per game led the Southeastern Conference and was seventh nationally.

But the carries were just the beginning.

With Jacobs' successful return from a hamstring injury the group was finally at full strength for the first time. In addition to Harris and junior Bo Scarbrough, there's true freshmen Najee Harris and Brian Robinson, plus junior Ronnie Clark scored his first career touchdown after coming back from two torn Achilles injuries.

That kind of mix wouldn't work at a lot of places, with egos getting in the way and players fighting for touches.

Not with these guys. Even though they have very different personalities—Jimmy Fallon could have a field day with his superlatives segment on the "Tonight Show" with this bunch—everyone's contributing.

"Damien, uh, he's goofy. He's definitely goofy, always trying to make jokes. But he's cool," said Jacobs, then adding after Harris left the room: "He's kind of like a big brother really.

"Damien would probably be class clown. Bo would probably be the hype man. Brian Robinson would be the sleeper. And Najee would probably be chill."

Their differences and versatility translated to the field, demonstrating both power and speed, with the blocking and receiving abilities to match.

For example, the coaches could insert Robinson as a fullback, Jones as a change-of-pace back, line up someone wide, or put two running backs in the backfield to really confuse the defense about what's coming.

They could also call for something specific, like

Damien Harris signals a first down during the Sugar Bowl semifinal against Clemson. Harris rushed 19 times for 77 yards in the Alabama win.

on the first play of the Arkansas game. The play was a sweep to the right, but Harris was looking for a big hole on the cutback if the Razorbacks over-pursued. They did, and he went 75 yards for the touchdown.

We haven't even gotten to arguably Alabama's most dangerous player in the running game, sophomore quarterback Jalen Hurts.

You always hear about how offenses can get a defense on its heels by having balance between the ground game and the passing attack because they don't know what's coming. Well, Alabama could do something similar with its rushing alone, especially when factoring in the quarterback.

If a defense spied someone over the top, he became a decoy. An interior linebacker cleared out on a fake or to pick someone up in coverage and Hurts had an easy first down. You get the idea.

Even with his sack yards, which count against rushing totals at the collegiate level, Hurts still challenged for the team rushing lead.

For much of the season Scarbrough had more touches, but Harris led in rushing yards. Consequently, Nick Saban described him as being the Crimson Tide's most consistent player on offense, with junior wide receiver Calvin Ridley second.

It really showed in his yards per carry average of 8.2 during the regular season, while Hurts was among the national rushing leaders among quarterback by averaging 5.6.

To put both figures into perspective consider that the Alabama record for yards per carry is 6.5, set by Eddie Lacy in 2012 (1,322 yards on 204 attempts). That's with a minimum of 200 attempts, while for 100 attempts the mark is 7.5 by Bobby Marlow in 1950 (882 yards, 118 attempts).

Want to take a guess at who was second behind Marlow? Damien Harris at 7.1, set in 2016 (1,037 yards, 46 attempts).

Hurts was also closing in fast on the Alabama career record for rushing yards by a quarterback. Crimson Tide legend Harry Gilmer had 2,025 from 1944-47, while the 19-year-old Hurts finished the 2017 regular season with 1,722.

In case you're wondering, Gilmer averaged 5.2 yards per carry.

So one way or another, Alabama's running game was too much for most defenses to handle, especially during the first half of the season. It had 496 rushing yards at Vanderbilt, 365 against Ole Miss, 232 at Texas A&M and 308 versus Arkansas. That's 1,401 yards and 17 touchdowns on the ground, during which the Crimson Tide defense yielded 226 and one score.

It worked out to a difference of nearly 300 yards per game, 350.2-56.5.

Nevertheless, the number to watch with Alabama's running game was still 140. When the Crimson Tide topped that in rushing yards it was 101-6 since 2008.

"That's kind of what we take pride in in whoever's number's called to being able to make the play," Harris said. "We don't care who makes it, as long as the play is made when it needs to be." ■

Josh Jacobs was an important part of the vaunted Alabama backfield in 2017, returning from an early season hamstring injury to provide a nice change of pace from the other backs.

ALABAMA 24, LSU 10

NOVEMBER 4, 2017 · TUSCALOOSA, ALABAMA

PASSING THE TEST

Tide Overcome Injuries to Top Tigers

No one could again say that this Alabama football team hadn't been tested enough. Critics could look at the rankings and the scores and draw whatever conclusions they wanted. But when it came to facing a talented, gutsy, and physical opponent, while also having to compensate for numerous injuries, Alabama's game against LSU was more than your typical brutal, grind-it-out game that this series had become known for.

Alabama won 24-10 for its seventh straight win against the Tigers, and the outcome was really never in doubt.

However, it turned into nothing short of a survival test for the No. 2 Crimson Tide, which also got a dose of humility handled to it earlier in the week with the College Football Playoff committee placing Georgia first in its initial rankings.

"Obviously a tough game," Nick Saban said. "I told the players before the game that we haven't been tested with hard. Hard is how they define you in terms of who you are. We didn't play a great game out there we had a lot of self-inflicted wounds, but you can't argue with the fight that the players fought with.

"They hung in there and did what they had to do to win."

Alabama's best defensive player, junior defensive back Minkah Fitzpatrick, suffered what appeared to be a hamstring injury early on. Starting senior interior linebacker Shaun Dion Hamilton (knee) was likely done for the season and reserve linebacker Mack Wilson (foot) would be sidelined for a while.

Of course, that's on top of linebackers Christian Miller and Terrell Lewis suffering major injuries in the season opener against Florida State. Senior Rashaan Evans, who had a painful groin injury against the Seminoles, tweaked his ankle. Sophomore Anfernee Jennings was wearing a walking boot after the game. Sophomore Mekhi Brown appeared to endure a painful a shoulder injury and junior Jamey Mosley left the game for a while with a knee injury, but did return.

All of them except for Evans were outside linebackers. Alabama played a lot of nickel, which only required three linebackers, but freshmen Dylan Moses and VanDarius Cowan and sophomore Joshua McMillon were all pressed into service.

"He's one of my dear friends," Evans said about Hamilton. "The way that it ended up the way that it did is a blow to our team.

"All we can do right now is continue to coach up these younger guys."

Nick Saban and the Crimson Tide prevailed over LSU once again but endured devastating injuries to the defense in the process, with Shaun Dion Hamilton and Mack Wilson going down for extended stretches.

PLAY OF THE GAME:

The key to Alabama's final touchdown drive was on third-and-9 at the LSU 40, when rolling to his right sophomore quarterback Jalen Hurts fired in a 15-yard pass to senior wide receiver Cam Sims, who was surrounded by four defenders. Three plays later, Alabama reached the end zone for a 21-3 lead.

PLAYERS OF THE GAME:

Senior punter JK Scott averaged 51.6 yards, including six inside the 20, and three of his five kickoffs were for touchbacks. LSU's best field position to start a drive was at its own 39-yard line, which ended on the first snap due to junior safety Ronnie Harrison's interception. Honorable mentions go to senior linebacker Rashaan Evans and quarterback Jalen Hurts.

Although Alabama jumped out to an early 14-0 lead, with one impressive touchdown drive and junior safety Ronnie Harrison stepping in front of a short pass for an interception to give his team first down at the LSU 37, statistically the Crimson Tide did anything but dominate.

LSU outgained Alabama 306-299.

It had the ball longer, 34:07-25:53.

It was better on third downs, especially in the first half, and went 9-for-19 in conversions compared to 5-for-14 for Alabama.

The Tigers even won the key stat that had been in favor of the winning team in every game in the recent rivalry except one, 2008, average rushing yards per carry — averaging 3.6 yards per carry to the Crimson Tide's 3.2.

"I don't think that was Alabama football," junior running back Bo Scarbrough said. "We should been more prepared. We should have done a way better job than we did. A lot of mental errors. A lot of mistakes that we have to fix.

"I don't think it had anything to do with the bye week."

Alabama's offensive line also had trouble with LSU's pass rush, which notched seven tackles for a loss, including four sacks and three hurries, while the Tigers also broke up seven passes. That's even more telling considering Alabama sophomore quarterback Jalen Hurts only attempted 24 passes, completing 10 — and had three dropped.

The Alabama defense converges on LSU running back Darrel Williams. Williams had 83 yards rushing and a touchdown in the game

Calvin Ridley had three catches for 61 yards in Alabama's seventh straight win over LSU.

STAT OF THE GAME:

LSU's average field position for the entire game was at its own 19. The Tigers crossed midfield only three times.

But Hurts still passed for 183 yards, including his 4-yard touchdown to sophomore tight end Irv Smith Jr., and ran for 44 more even though LSU stacked the box.

"Our defense picked us up," senior center Bradley Bozeman said. "We have to get better."

Alabama did slow LSU running back Derrius Guice, who had 71 yards on 19 carries (3.7), with his longest carry just nine yards, and five receptions for 29 yards.

However, Darrell Williams out of the wildcat busted a 54-yard gain that led to LSU's first touchdown against Alabama since 2015.

Saban credited the gaffe to a check off a shift, with only half of the defense making the adjustment, but it was also shortly after Hamilton's injury and when junior defensive tackle Da'Ron Payne was being spelled.

Alabama still finished with a season-high six sacks, including Moses notching one on LSU's final snap, to give him 1.5 for the game.

Alabama's going to need a lot more from players like him, because just like this turned into a survival test, now the rest of the season is as well for the 9-0 Crimson Tide.

"You gotta prove it every week," Jennings said. ∎

ALABAMA 31, MISSISSIPPI STATE 24
NOVEMBER 11, 2017 · STARKVILLE, MISSISSIPPI

THEY FINISHED
Crimson Tide Executes Late to Survive Close Call in Starkville

Clutch.

There's no other way to describe Alabama's 31-24 victory at Davis Wade Stadium.

When the game was on the line, No. 2 Alabama made the plays and No. 16 Mississippi State did not. That's a bit of an oversimplification, but only a small one considering that the Crimson Tide scored two touchdowns in the final quarter to remain undefeated.

"My heartbeat's still going about 120 miles per hour," sophomore left tackle Jonah Williams said afterward, and he wasn't the only one.

This was as good of a test as the Crimson Tide's had all year, and Alabama came oh-so-close to not passing. Between the LSU hangover and not having senior linebacker Shaun Dion Hamilton, whose absence after suffering a season-ending knee injury was obvious, Mississippi State caught it at the right time and had it in the right place.

Thanks in part to two Alabama penalties that helped extend two early Bulldog possessions, Mississippi State played ball control and keep away, with an early time of possession edge of 11:12-3:48. The Crimson Tide countered with big plays.

For example, after the Bulldogs opened the scoring with an 11-yard touchdown by running back Aeris Williams, Alabama needed just 114 seconds to counter with a 63-yard gain by junior wide receiver Calvin Ridley, setting up a 1-yard touchdown run by sophomore quarterback Jalen Hurts.

It set the tone for the back-and-forth nature of the night.

Coming in, Alabama hadn't allowed a touchdown in the first quarter of any game this season, and none in the first half against an SEC opponent. It yielded two to the Bulldogs, both to Williams on the ground, en route to a 14-14 halftime score.

Alabama managed just 40 rushing yards as a team at the break while MSU had 99 against a defense that had averaged 75.8 per game.

"The defense needs to get their own rest sometimes," Nick Saban said. "They went eight for 15 on third down. We didn't do a very good job of getting off the field on third down. A myriad of mistakes, guys losing contain, guys blitzing when they're not supposed to blitz, not doing a good job of covering sometimes. Lots of things to correct."

Senior linebacker Rashaan Evans said, "We just kind of had to pull together and play as a team." But it didn't happen until the fourth quarter.

Alabama defensive back Hootie Jones (6) knocks away a pass by Mississippi State quarterback Nick Fitzgerald in the end zone in the final seconds of the dramatic Alabama win.

PLAY OF THE GAME: Alabama's last two offensive plays were slant passes that beat the blitz. The first, on third-and-15 to junior wide receiver Calvin Ridley, set up the second, freshman Devonta Smith's 26-yard touchdown with 25 seconds remaining.

PLAYERS OF THE GAME:

Sophomore quarterback Jalen Hurts and junior wide receiver Calvin Ridley. Ridley finished with five receptions for 171 yards and Hurts accounted for 108 yards of total offense in the fourth quarter when the game was on the line.

At the time Mississippi State was coming off its feel-good "Don't Stop Believing" moment when the fans use their cell phones to light up the stands, and the Bulldogs were leading 24-17. They had worn down the Alabama defense (time of possession was up to 33:31-11:29) and had the momentum.

That's when this Alabama team may have found out what it's made of.

It began with sophomore running back Josh Jacobs igniting the ground game, which had been outgained 160-82. He and Hurts keyed a 10-play drive with junior running back Damien Harris scoring on a 14-yard run that not only tied the game, but gave the defense a chance to regroup.

The possession was even more impressive considering that Mississippi State had three players suffer injuries and the Bulldogs called two timeouts, which kept breaking up the Crimson Tide's tempo. Alabama also went for it on fourth-and-4 at the MSU 34, with Hurts running for the critical first down.

Mississippi State's answer was a five-play, 18-yard possession that fizzled at midfield.

With the ball and just 6:30 remaining, Alabama drove only to see senior kicker Andy Pappanastos' 41-yard field-goal attempt clang off the left upright. Yet again it gave the defense some recovery time on the sideline. It subsequently forced its lone three-and-out of the night, setting up Alabama's final possession with 1:09 remaining.

This time Hurts went to the air, finding Ridley for a 15-yard gain to get the drive going, and again for 31 yards on third-and-15 at the Alabama 43.

"He changed the play and gave me a slant," Ridley said about Hurts. "He does the little things that we need."

Damien Harris fends off the Mississippi State defender, part of a strong day rushing with 93 yards and a touchdown.

STAT OF THE GAME:

Alabama outgained Mississippi State 192-34 in the fourth quarter.

The 26-yard pass to freshman Devonta Smith completed the 68-yard drive and comeback, although Alabama still flirted with disaster. JK Scott's kickoff went out of bounds and Mississippi State got two tries at a Hail Mary when the first was flagged for pass interference.

No matter.

Ridley finished with five receptions for 171 yards and Hurts was 10-for-19 for 242 yards and the one touchdown pass. Despite having the ball for just 21:04, Alabama still managed 444 total yards.

"It kind of felt like Clemson," said senior cornerback Anthony Averett, with numerous teammates agreeing that the game reminded them of the previous season's national championship.

There was one obvious and important difference, though.

"We finished," he said. ■

Above: Nick Saban found a lot to critique in the win, but Alabama improved to a perfect 10-0 in the process. Opposite: Junior tight end Hale Hentges hauls in a pass, his lone catch in the Alabama win.

PLAYMAKERS
Evans and Fitzpatrick Bring Adaptability to Crimson Tide Defense

It was a direct question to Alabama senior linebacker Rashaan Evans that caused him to pause and let out an "ooh."

Who's a more versatile player on the Crimson Tide defense, Evans or junior defensive back Minkah Fitzpatrick?

Even Evans wasn't sure.

"Minkah's very fast, fast twitch-type guy, just as much as I am," Evans said. "With us, I feel like if we changed sizes, we could play each other's position.

"Just with the type of guy he is, we compare a lot. He's a guy that he's one of those leaders on our team and he can make big time plays just as much as I can."

Although they may not play the same positions or have the same build, as Fitzpatrick (6'1", 202 pounds) is a defensive back and Evans (6'3", 234) is clearly a front-seven player, between the two of them they could line up just about anywhere.

Evans is an interior linebacker in the base package, knows the outside linebacker spots and can play there at any time, and often moves up to the line as a pass-rusher.

Fitzpatrick has played cornerback, safety, and both additional spots in the nickel and dime packages, known in Nick Saban's scheme as the star and money positions (the key is the first letter, with the star replacing the strong-side linebacker and the money subbing for the middle linebacker). Defensive coordinator Jeremy Pruitt has also used him as a disruptive blitzer.

"I'm good," he said about the additional wear and tear. "I'm always in the training room either getting iced up, stretched, massaged. I just try to take advantage of it."

They also both play on special teams and Evans has emerged as a team leader while taking over the spot previously held by Butkus Award winner Reuben Foster.

"He came a long way from last year, as far as a leadership role goes," sophomore outside linebacker Anfernee Jennings said. "He knew he had to step up."

Consequently, the two might be the biggest playmakers on the talented Crimson Tide defense. Although Evans sustained a groin injury by trying to return a blocked field goal by Fitzpatrick in the season opener against Florida State, he's now coming on strong and is moving up among Alabama's statistical leaders.

He's tied for the lead in tackles for a loss (6) and is second in sacks to defensive lineman Raekwon Davis (3). He's also second in quarterback hurries to Isaiah Buggs.

It's that ability that led linebacker coach Tosh Lupoi to start calling Evans "Razor" last year.

"I like to cut," Evans said about playing the edge.

It was while filling in for injured Shaun Dion Hamilton at the end of last year that Evans gave a taste of his potential, with a career-high seven tackles, including a sack, against Washington in the College Football Playoff semifinal. He then topped that with 11 tackles against Clemson in the National Championship Game.

But this season he's obviously not standing in for anyone, and while coaches had to be careful with his injury and rehabilitation to minimize the risk of a setback, he got closer to full strength with each passing week.

Rashaan Evans works through drills during practice at the Thomas-Drew Practice Fields. The senior linebacker is an indispensable member of the intimidating Alabama defense.

The combination could make things very difficult for opponents.

"Coach Saban's big on affecting the quarterback, disrupting the quarterback and doing all those things," sophomore quarterback Jalen Hurts said. "So if Minkah or Rashaan or whoever's on the edge, just switching it around a little bit, if that's going to affect the quarterback then that's what we're going to do sometimes."

You often hear about defensive players who are so good that the quarterback has to be aware of where they are before every snap, although in reality they're pretty rare. Derwin James was like that for Hurts against Florida State, while Fitzpatrick has been just as a versatile for the Crimson Tide.

Nick Saban gave an indication of how valuable he's been before facing the potent Ole Miss offense:

"Having a guy like Minkah really in a game like this really helps it because there are a lot of matchup issues," the coach said. "When they have four or five receivers

Above: Minkah Fitzpatrick, winner of the Chuck Bednarik Award for defensive player of the year, poses with the trophy during the College Football Awards show at the College Football Hall of Fame in Atlanta. Opposite: Fitzpatrick smiles during warm-ups prior to the Allstate Sugar Bowl against the Clemson Tigers. Fitzpatrick had three tackles in the win, including a tackle for loss.

on the field, if you play five defensive backs that's probably not enough. If you play six, maybe you match up a little bit better. But maybe you have some other issues when it comes to other things you want to defend. So when you have players like Minkah, it gives you the diversity to do some of these things.

"He's very good at it because of the adaptability. He's smart, he can learn multiple tasks with minimal reps."

Evans could have a similar presence, maybe not as much in the passing game, but equally disruptive, which could be crucial against top competition.

Communication was the key. So at times you'd see quick counter adjustments, not just to react but to give players like Evans and Fitzpatrick a better opportunity to make big plays from all over the field.

After all, they were so much alike … except when it came to their hair. Given time, though, Evans believes he could pull off his teammates' upright style.

"I don't know if he could pull off the bald, though," he said. "That would be interesting to see." ◼

Above: Minkah Fitzpatrick hits the arm of Vanderbilt quarterback Kyle Shurmur to cause an incomplete pass in Alabama's 59-0 rout. Opposite: Rashaan Evans looks to pressure Clemson quarterback Kelly Bryant during the College Football Playoff Semifinal. Evans powered the Crimson Tide in the win with nine tackles and a sack.

ALABAMA 56, MERCER 0

NOVEMBER 18, 2017 · TUSCALOOSA, ALABAMA

SENIORS STRONG

Bama Dominates Mercer Home Finale

Jessica Carr made the trip.

If you didn't know the story, or any of what she's been through, you probably wouldn't have noticed her during Alabama's pregame Senior Day ceremony. She was toward the middle of the long line of players and families being honored, alongside her son, defensive back Hootie Jones.

It was the first time Carr had been able to make one of his games at Bryant-Denny Stadium.

He then went out and got an interception for Mama.

"I just want to thank her for being here," the senior safety said.

It was a memorable day for both Jones and the Crimson Tide, which crushed FCS opponent Mercer 56-0 before a thunderstorm blew through the area. One could argue that Alabama was just as powerful on the football field, outgaining the Bears 530-161 despite pulling starters early in the second quarter. But that's not what the day was ultimately about.

Sophomore quarterback Jalen Hurts completed all seven of his attempts for 180 yards and three touchdowns. His top target, junior wide receiver Calvin Ridley, had three catches for 103 yards including a 66-yard touchdown, and then called it a day.

No. 1 Alabama also worked on some contingency plans. It slid sophomore left tackle Jonah Williams to left guard to insert freshman Alex Leatherwood in case junior Ross Pierschbacher (ankle) remained sidelined. Senior punter JK Scott kicked extra points and sophomore running back Joshua Jacobs was a kick returner.

Yet the day belonged the seniors and their families, especially those who may not always be in the limelight.

Guys like Jones.

Some fans know Jones for his brightly-dyed hair, initially the result of a bet with a friend from home. Others only heard about his getting arrested on drug and weapons charges when he and Cam Robinson were sitting in a car late one night in their hometown of Monroe, Louisiana, last year.

Charges were eventually dropped, but the stigma stuck around, especially since many of the hometown fans were still holding a grudge that he had left to play college ball.

But there was always a lot more under the surface with Jones.

Carr had been battling stage 4 lymphoma for most of her son's collegiate career. At one point Jones considered transferring to Louisiana Monroe or Louisiana Tech to help out more. Instead, he started washing cars at a dealership after games and practices

Freshman quarterback Tua Tagovailoa threw for 85 yards and three touchdowns in the shutout win over Mercer.

PLAY OF THE GAME:

It's not very often one sees a wide receiver make a move that's so good the defender falls to the ground, but junior Calvin Ridley did so on his 66-yard touchdown off a play-action.

PLAYER OF THE GAME:
He missed some assignments and reads, but true freshman linebacker Dylan Moses was all over the field. He was credited with 11 tackles, 10 solo, including four for a loss. Moses also made an interception in the red zone and the tackle on 4th-and-4 in the third quarter to snuff out Mercer's two best drives.

to make a few extra dollars to send home while continuing to work on his degree.

Jones stuck it out, and his mother, who was doing better, was able to make the trip when he walked at graduation in August.

This was just gravy.

"It was pretty big for him," senior wide receiver Cam Sims said.

It was for Sims as well, who had been through the whole experience with Jones, even before his friend agonized over whether to attend Alabama or LSU. He and Robinson had been there in the auditorium at Neville High School when Jones announced he was following them to Tuscaloosa.

They may be even tighter now.

"It really hit me when we had to go out there and introduce the seniors," Sims said. "I almost shed a tear. But when I saw my mom out there I had to focus up and help her kind of calm down. Then the game came and I had to kind of hit that switch."

So did Jones, a key contributor in the nickel and dime packages who started in place of injured strong safety Minkah Fitzpatrick (hamstring). He wasn't often challenged as Mercer's longest completion ended up being just 13 yards, but the interception came early in the second quarter just before Nick Saban started to pull the starters.

Bears quarterback Kaelan Riley, whose team was already in a 21-0 hole, tried to make something happen on first-and-10 at his own 25, with Jones snaring the ball at the 40. It took the Crimson Tide offense only three plays to reach the end zone, on Jacobs' 7-yard shovel pass from Hurts.

"Before the game, he was like 'We have to do something to go out strong,'" Sims said. "When he

caught that pick, I was 'He's doing something big.' I was really happy for him."

Sims' turn came in the third quarter, an 8-yard touchdown throw from freshman Tua Tagovailoa. Ironically, he was the only senior to reach the end zone for the Crimson Tide, although anyone who was eligible dressed and just about everyone got into the game.

"This senior class has been phenomenal," Saban said. "They were walking out for the second half and saying: 'This is the last time I'm going to walk down this tunnel with you.' I'm glad to see them do well. They played well today."

Sims called the final game both "Sad and happy at the same time," and Jones said the whole day just gave him a "great feeling."

Yet the season wasn't over yet. With 51 wins the senior class had only tied the NCAA record set by the previous year's Crimson Tide, and wanted to add to its ring collection of three SEC titles and one national championship.

The next step was at Auburn, where Jones wasn't ready to speculate on whether teammates Christian Miller and Terrell Lewis might be ready to join the Crimson Tide for the Iron Bowl after being out for 10 games.

"Hey man, we got a lot of secrets packed in our bag," he said. "We don't let none of that get out there until it's out there." ∎

Tight end Hale Hentges, left, celebrates with Irv Smith Jr. after scoring a touchdown during the first half of Alabama's 56-0 Senior Day win.

STAT OF THE GAME:
Alabama needed just four possessions to top Auburn's point total against Mercer earlier this season. The Crimson Tide averaged 12.6 yards per snap and they collectively took 7:53 of game time.

IRON BOWL

AUBURN 26, ALABAMA 14

NOVEMBER 25, 2017 · AUBURN, ALABAMA

DERAILED

Surging Tigers Topple Undefeated Tide

As the leaders of the Alabama football team met with reporters in the hallway outside of their locker room at Jordan-Hare Stadium, the scene behind them with their teammates in the parking lot told the story.

There were tears, disbelieving faces, and consoling hugs from friends and family. Senior safety Hootie Jones was helped into an ambulance after sustaining a season-ending left knee injury, while the rest of the Crimson Tide slowly boarded the team busses.

Mostly, no one knew how to act. The No. 1 Crimson Tide had rattled off 11-straight victories before seeing their season possibly derailed, 26-14. Nobody on the roster had ever experienced a loss by more than seven points, dating back to the end of the 2013 season, the 45-31 defeat to Oklahoma in the Sugar Bowl.

This was all new to them. After three straight years of going to the SEC Championship, and winning in decisive fashion, the Crimson Tide had to wait and hope to back into the College Football Playoff for a fourth straight appearance.

"We didn't execute," said quarterback Jalen Hurts, who took just his second career loss as a starting quarterback.

As unusual as the situation was, so was how the Crimson Tide played against its biggest rival. There were mistakes galore and players looking like they had never been in a big game before, while No. 6 Auburn gave it everything it had.

Perhaps the perfect example of how uncharacteristically Alabama played came with about 10 minutes remaining when it didn't just have one bad snap, but two, on third and fourth down with the game on the line. They might have been the offense's first bad snaps of the season.

"There's no excuse when that happens," senior center Bradley Bozeman said.

"We were going clap," Saban explained about the silent count. "Bo (Scarbrough) said he heard someone clap, whether it was one of their players or one of our players, I'm not accusing anybody of anything.

"The second time, Bo clapped to try and get the line's attention. We weren't even set on the play. I thought they should have called illegal procedure on us."

Instead, Alabama got a second chance when Auburn was flagged for having too many men on the field. On fourth-and-4, Hurts found senior wide receiver Robert Foster. Instead of doing everything he could to get the first down, Foster went for extra yards and was subsequently dropped after just 3.

Calvin Ridley stretches to catch a pass against Auburn. The Tigers' defense limited the Crimson Tide's receivers to just 13 receptions and 103 yards.

PLAY OF THE GAME:
The longest play by either side was the 36-yard touchdown reception by freshman wide receiver Jerry Jeudy. Junior wide receiver Calvin Ridley appeared to be the intended target, but when sophomore quarterback Jalen Hurts couldn't get him the ball he took a shot at the end zone that paid off.

PLAYERS OF THE GAME:

Ronnie Harrison and Da'Ron Payne. Harrison was credited with seven tackles, including the hard hit on running back Kerryon Johnson to keep him out of the end zone, while Payne had a fumble recovery and hurry to go with three tackles.

It was that kind of night all around.

Auburn quarterback Jarrett Stidham was 21 for 28 for 237 yards and sacked only once despite facing constant pressure. He had 12 completions in the first quarter alone, which no opponent had previously done during the Saban era at Alabama.

Running back Kerryon Johnson tallied 104 rushing yards on 30 carries before leaving with a shoulder injury. He also threw a 3-yard jump pass for a touchdown out of the wildcat to cap a 12-play, 95-yard drive after Alabama elected not to go for it on fourth-and-1 at the Auburn 48 in the first quarter.

Coming in, Alabama had converted every fourth-down opportunity this season.

But the statistic that best demonstrated the difference between the teams was third-down conversions.

Alabama was just 3 for 11, while Auburn was 9 of 18. The Tigers were clutch when it mattered and the Crimson Tide was not.

"For us, we just needed to get off the field on third down," senior linebacker Rashaan Evans said. "We didn't do a good job of that."

"We weren't very good," said Saban, and he meant both sides of the ball.

The only time Alabama had the lead was at the start of the second half. After the Crimson Tide had just five carries by the running backs in the first half, it carved up the Tigers with an 80-yard drive capped by junior Bo Scarbrough's 21-yard touchdown.

"We came out with a little fire, a little intensity, right out of halftime and had a great drive," Saban said. "We just couldn't sustain it."

Tailback Bo Scarbrough had six carries for 46 yards and a touchdown against Auburn.

STAT OF THE GAME:

Alabama converted just 3 of 11 third-down opportunities, while Auburn was 9 of 18.

That was it for the Crimson Tide. The next time it got close to scoring, holder JK Scott had the ball slip out of his hand on a field-goal attempt. He had the presence of mind to throw a pass, but the swarming Tigers snuffed it, and the Crimson Tide, out.

"I don't know," said Minkah Fitzpatrick when asked how he'd spend this upcoming week with the team not heading to Atlanta for the SEC Championship Game. "We're not used to this." ■

Above: Nick Saban paces on the Alabama sideline during the Iron Bowl. Opposite: Auburn defenders swarm Alabama running back Josh Jacobs. Alabama struggled against the Tigers' defense all afternoon.

QUARTERBACK
JALEN HURTS
Sophomore Hurts Turns Pain into Passion

The photo was on his cell phone for a long time, to serve as both a reminder and motivation.

It was of Clemson celebrating with the national championship trophy after defeating Alabama, 35-31. Jalen Hurts had run in what would have been a game-winning touchdown on nearly any other night, only to see the Tigers top it with one second remaining.

The feeling was something that he never wanted to forget.

"When you lose to a team, you like to get another chance to play them again," Hurts said about his first loss at the collegiate level. "That's like when you're playing your big brother in NCAA and he kind of (gets) after you the first time. You want to play him again.

"I think everybody likes a second chance."

Yes, Alabama got one, both in terms of still having a shot at the national championship and some possible payback in the Sugar Bowl semifinal. A year after Clemson was able to avenge the previous national title game, Alabama wanted nothing more than to return the favor after squeezing into the College Football Playoff.

The selection committee granted it the opportunity after finishing the regular season 11-1, even though it meant selecting a second team from one conference for the first time.

Afterward, justifying the committee's decision wasn't so much on Alabama's radar – it felt it belonged despite not having played for the Southeastern Conference championship. Even so, there were far bigger concerns including what's at stake and the task at hand.

Clemson was the top-seeded team in the tournament, not Alabama.

"You don't want to dwell on the past and we don't want to get caught up in this being an emotional game, like they beat us last year so we have to do something different in order to beat them this year," Hurts said. "I mean in the offseason, I think that really fueled us. Our whole motto was finishing.

"But now, we're just focused on us and we're focused on playing our best football."

What's different, though, was Alabama became the first playoff team that was coming off a loss, 26-14 to its biggest rival. The Crimson Tide's regular-season dud finale at Auburn lingered, if not festered, for three weeks until the players got back on the field and could start to do something about it.

However, the fans didn't have that luxury. They

Quarterback Jalen Hurts was all smiles after Alabama topped Clemson in the Sugar Bowl to avenge their loss to the Tigers' in the College Football Playoff championship game the previous season.

kept looking at and dwelling on statistics like Hurts having as many rushing attempts as the top three running backs combined against Auburn (18), plus the third-down struggles, plus the plain fact that Alabama lost.

No one cared that Hurts' passer-efficiency rating of 155.6 was a major improvement over the previous season, and he finished the regular season ranked 12th in the nation in that category (his 139.1 rating as a freshman ranked 44th in the nation despite being regularly boosted by Alabama's shovel passes that were glorified handoffs to wide receivers on jet sweeps). Or that he obviously had better command of the offense, and only one interception during the regular season.

Neither did he.

"I ain't perfect," Hurts said. "Far from that. I live and I learn.

"Michael Jordan said that the other day. You don't lose, you learn. I don't lose, I learn. I think we've learned from a lot of things this year. Even last year's loss. How can we show the world we've learned? How far have we (come)? I think we're trying to get better right now. We're learning from it and trying to continue to improve and show it on New Year's Day."

That even-keeled nature is probably what Hurts is known for most of all. He doesn't get too excited, nor too down—although he did sport both a Houston Astros shirt and a big smile around campus after they won the World Series.

Earlier in the season Hurts didn't want to be the story, or a distraction, when Alabama headed to Texas A&M shortly after Hurricane Harvey decimated the area. College State is about a 90-minute drive inland from his hometown of Houston, where 40-61 inches of rain fell in a region that usually gets that much over a whole year, and 130-mph winds took their toll. The devastating storm was credited with 84 deaths (not all in Texas), and governor Greg Abbott estimated the damage to be between $150-$180 billion in his state alone.

Jalen Hurts (right) and defensive lineman Da'Ron Payne raise the championship trophy following Alabama's win over Clemson in the Allstate Sugar Bowl semifinal.

"At the end of the day, it's another game," he said. "A tough road environment that we have to play in and we have to be ready."

At least he got to see his family and friends, but not the devastation. It was still a business trip.

In a parallel universe somewhere, Hurts probably started the game for the other side as Texas A&M and Mississippi State were finalists for his signature as a recruit. Previously he had longed to play for Texas, having grown up watching Vince Young, but his preferred team was smitten with another quarterback.

His father, the head coach at Channelview High School, described it to 247Sports as being like a "girlfriend that broke your heart."

It forced his son to grow up some, and maybe contributed to the remarkable poise that helped the true freshman win the Crimson Tide's starting job just after turning 18.

"Jalen's played really well for us," Saban said. "We're really pleased with the progress that he's made. We wanted to do a little better job, maybe, developing him in the passing game, and I think we've done that.

"Obviously, we still have room to improve—I'm not talking just about Jalen, but I'm talking about as an overall team, so that we have the kind of balance that we need. But he's been a good decision-maker and played very well, kept his eyes downfield and has made some nice plays in the passing game."

Hurts eventually did stop looking at the celebratory photo, but only because he got a new phone. Yet the replacement had the same sentiment and also served as a reminder to focus on himself. It was of him walking off the field at Raymond James Stadium.

"I don't look at it like, 'Dang, I lost to Clemson.' I don't do that every time," he said. "But it's definitely there, it's definitely a motivating factor and it's always been."

Of course, you know what he planned to do with that photo after facing Clemson again.

"Hopefully I can remove it," he said. ■

Jalen Hurts throws a touchdown pass to 308-pound defensive tackle Da'Ron Payne to give Alabama a 17-6 lead in the third quarter of the Sugar Bowl.

SUGAR BOWL

ALABAMA 24, CLEMSON 6

JANUARY 1, 2018 · NEW ORLEANS, LOUISIANA

THE BIG EASY

Alabama Dominates Clemson to Reach Championship Game

Welcome back, Alabama.

Not necessarily to the National Championship Game, where it'll be making its third straight appearance and sixth under Nick Saban in nine years. Or for making it an all-Southeastern Conference affair again, as Georgia won its roller-coaster Rose Bowl semifinal against Oklahoma earlier in the day.

Rather, welcome back to playing Crimson Tide-style football.

After hearing nothing for a month about how it had lost its last game to Auburn and lost in the last second a year earlier to Clemson and how it had sort of lost its way, Alabama had had enough.

It played physical. It was relentless. It made the big plays. And it won round three against the Tigers after splitting the last two national championships. Unlike those games, though, this one wasn't close.

Finally playing the style of football it preferred against Dabo Swinney's team following two shootouts, Alabama treated Clemson like a dog does a toy, wildly shaking it while the stuffing spewed out for a 24-6 victory in the Sugar Bowl.

"Tonight was about our identity as a team," Nick Saban said. "I don't think anyone can question the relentless competitive attitude that we played with, a warrior-like mentality out there.

"It was a little personal to us."

It was also almost like a tip of the hat to some of Alabama's other recent championship teams, and not just because similar to its last win at the Mercedes-Benz Superdome, at the end of the 2011 season against LSU, the defense kept the opposition out of the end zone.

Alabama came out reminding fans of the 2009 team that pummeled Florida in the SEC Championship Game — a game known as "Tim Tebow wept" — and the 2012 national champions that pounded Notre Dame.

But it was a play similar to the 2009 title game against Texas that foretold the outcome. As if invoking the spirit of Marcell Dareus, Alabama defensive tackle Da'Ron Payne's interception in the third quarter started an emotional avalanche that smothered the Tigers.

"I was just surprised I had the ball," Payne said about his 21-yard return.

He didn't reach the end zone on the return, but did

Linebacker Terrell Lewis runs onto the field signaling a play during Alabama's 24-6 win over Clemson in the Sugar Bowl.

PLAY OF THE GAME:

Take your pick between junior defensive lineman Da'Ron Payne's interception and his subsequent touchdown. However, there's something to be said about how after a year of hearing critics claim that Clemson's pick/rub play to score the game-winning touchdown with one second remaining in the national championship was legal, Alabama essentially ran the same play with two defensive linemen.

Before he got hurt, sophomore outside linebacker Anfernee Jennings made five tackles including three for a loss, and had a sack against Clemson's best offensive lineman, left tackle Mitch Hyatt. Those don't include the hit he made on quarterback Kelly Bryant to cause the ball to go to Payne for his interception.

a few plays later. In the jumbo package, which included two defensive linemen as fullbacks, Payne bounced to his right like he had before in motion, only with the snap didn't plow into the line. He followed sophomore Quinnen Williams out to the right, caught the lob pass, and got two feet down for the pile-driving touchdown.

It might have been the first time in the history of college football that the offensive player of a bowl game threw a touchdown to the defensive player of the game.

"When he made the interception, there was no doubt that we were going to throw him the ball at the goal line," Saban quipped.

However, Alabama wasn't done yet. Clemson's first snap following the kickoff was deflected by senior cornerback Levi Wallace, with the ball going to sophomore linebacker Mack Wilson. He went 18 yards and dove for the pylon for just the Crimson Tide's second defensive touchdown of the season.

All that after Alabama gave Clemson numerous opportunities to get back in the game, including a missed a field goal at the end of the first half and lost a fumble on its first play after the break.

But the defense remained resolute. Paired with the offensive line getting sick of hearing of how the Clemson front four were the best in college football, Alabama won the game in the trenches, just like so many Crimson Tide teams before.

It grinded away, with junior running back Damien Harris, who had six carries in the Crimson Tide's last game at Auburn, taking 12 handoffs in the first half alone, and finishing with 19 attempts for 77 yards. Junior Bo Scarbrough was right behind him with 12 carries as Alabama ran the ball 42 times out of 66 plays.

Sophomore quarterback Jalen Hurts also completed 16 of 24 passes, but nothing longer than a 22-yard gain when freshman running back Najee Harris seemed to

Najee Harris pushes off Clemson safety Van Smith as he gains 22 yards and a first down in the second quarter.

The Clemson and Alabama lines prepare for the snap during the Sugar Bowl. The Crimson Tide limited the Tigers to just 188 yards of total offense and forced two turnovers in a dominant win over the defending national champion.

catch the Clemson defense by surprise. It was just his sixth reception of the season and first since Tennessee.

Alabama had a 182-73 advantage in total yards and 18:34-11:26 in time of possession while setting the tone in the first half. The Crimson Tide were even 5 for 9 on third-down conversions, but still only led 10-3 thanks to a 12-yard touchdown reception by Calvin Ridley.

It just needed a big play by a big man to get going.

"We dominated. We dominated. We dominated," Ridley said during the postgame celebration.

Alabama did. Plagued by horrible field position, Clemson had minus-7 yards in the first quarter. After executing 99 plays in last year's national championship, it had just 26 in the first half, when it managed just four first downs. It didn't fare any better in the second half, when Alabama killer Hunter Renfrow had all five of his receptions for just 31 yards.

The Tigers had a 20-yard run by quarterback Kelly Bryant in the first half, and two 19-yard receptions by wide receiver Deon Cain. Those three plays accounted for 31 percent of their total offense.

Meanwhile, Alabama broke up nine passes, notched five sacks, and led by sophomore linebacker Anfernee Jennings — who suffered a sprained knee late in the game — totaled nine tackles for a loss.

"They were the better team today," Clemson coach Dabo Swinney said. "No question about it."

Consequently, Saban notched his seventh career win against a No. 1 opponent, three more than anyone else in college football history. He moved on to face former assistant coach Kirby Smart and Georgia, a double-overtime 54-48 winner over Oklahoma in the Rose Bowl, in their Atlanta back yard.

But Alabama got some payback, and more.

"It was redemption," Hurts said. "We have been here before. We can't be too happy. We have to get ready to go out and finish this thing." ∎

Alabama tackle Jedrick Wills Jr. clears a path for running back Damien Harris. Harris led Alabama's rushing attack with 77 yards on 19 carries.